THE 8 CHARACTERISTICS OF THE
AWESOME ADJUSTER

BY

CARL VAN

*For my father, John Martin, who, through his love and giving,
taught me the two lessons to which I contribute all my success:
Always give more than you are asked; Being kind,
when you don't have to be, is the greatest strength there is.*

ACKNOWLEDGEMENTS

Without the support of some key customers, I would never have had the time or opportunity to write this book. I'd like to take the time to thank these especially loyal customers for their extraordinary support over the last few years:

Steve Rowland, Commercial Claims Administration Manager, Farmers Insurance
Ed Morris, Vice President of Claims Litigation, Farmers Insurance
Suzanne Wilson, Training Manager, Electric Insurance
Dianna Willey, Training Leader, Ohio Casualty
Dan Dudenhoefer, Group Vice President, Infinity Insurance
Teresa Ramos, Director of Education & Training, Mercury Insurance
Mike Turney, Director of Human Resourses, Mercury Insurance
Deborah Smith, Claims Director, Zurich Insurance
Giles Broucher, AVP Liability, Zurich Insurance
Leslie Burns, Customer Service Director, Zurich Insurance
Tom Schmitt, Human Resources Sr.VP, OneBeacon Insurance
Wendell Lambert, Claims Administrative Manager, Texas Farm Bureau
Steve Williams, Claims Vice President, Texas Farm Bureau
Mary Christian, Director of Training, Westfield Group
Rich Hernandez, Claims Vice President, Horace Mann
Jeff Horn, Claims Operations Analyst, Safeco Insurance
Connie Conlin, Regional Claims Manager, AAA of Michigan
Trevor Lomberg, Director of Claims Operations, Royal Bank of Canada
Richard Rieder, Regional Claim Specialist, American Family Insurance
Timothy Sprecher, Learning Director, American Family Insurance
Stann Rose, State Claims Manager, Progressive Insurance

I would like to thank Sue Tarrach for helping write the original article, and Brad Baumann who helped me start International Insurance Institute, Inc.

I would also like to thank my wife, Ann, for her love and support; my daughter Amanda, for our discussions of human behavior; and my step-daughters Molly and Layne who did most of the typing.

Table of Contents

Introduction

I consider myself a trainer, course designer, and coach . . . not a writer. So please forgive me if, during this book, I slip in and out of my trainer mode and, instead of just commenting on what Awesome Adjusters do, actually try to teach.

I prefer talking to people rather than writing to them. I love the phone, and hate e-mail. This is why I have chosen to write this book in the style of actually talking to someone. I will refer to you, the reader, in this book without having any idea who you are or what you do. That is to simply help me convey the concepts without tuning out. It helps me if I pretend I'm talking to someone rather than writing to them.

I mention this because I wouldn't want anyone to get mad at me and say to themselves, "What is he talking about, I don't do that." Just know that when I refer to "you," I'm talking to those of you who see the need for improvement and want help.

I freely use the word "we" throughout this book, because I want you to know I consider myself a claims person. No matter what project I may be working on, or any business endeavor I may be involved in, I NEVER forget that I am a claims person, and never want anyone else to forget it either. After all, I am not writing this book for TV repair people; I am writing it for claims folks. So I hope nobody minds that I fight to stay in the club.

Another thing you should know when reading this book, is that in most cases when I use names as customers and adjusters, that those are not the actual names of those adjusters and/or customers. They are the names of friends and family members. I decided this might increase the chance that at least someone might read this book if they knew their name was in it.

However, when I refer to actual Awesome Adjusters, and refer to them by name, rest assured that these people are real, and are out there right now being awesome. Some have since moved into claims management, and others love their jobs so much they stay right where they are.

CHAPTER 1

How the Search Began

I realize that this discussion would be better placed in the Introduction sec-tion of this book. However, most claims people are usually so busy, they cer-tainly would not have time to read an Introduction section. So here it is.

Among the many things I have done in my career, one of the most interest-ing was to be an auditor for a federal regulatory agency. My background in insurance gave me the opportunity to perform weeklong audits of claim operations.

One day I was working on an audit, when one of my fellow auditors said something to me that haunted me for a long time. He said, "Carl, you know, there really isn't very much difference between people." And I responded, "What do you mean there really isn't much difference; of course there is. Look at the quality of the work that this adjuster is doing versus this other adjuster. It's clear that there is a big difference between people." And his reply was, "Well, no not really. It's really the system that is important, not the workers themselves."

I continued to disagree with him until he asked me to consider something. He said, "Let's say you're going to race Jeff Gordon, and let's say I put him in a VW bug and you in a Corvette. Who would win the race?"

I said, "Well of course, I would." And he said, "Right, that's because you have a better system. Even though he is a better driver, it's the system that makes the difference, and you will ultimately out perform him because you have a much better system. Now, if we put you both in the same car, of course he would win. Either both in the VW bug or both in the Corvette, he would win. But it wouldn't take a car much faster than a VW bug for you to beat Jeff Gordon. Once again, that's because there isn't very much difference between people; it's the system that's important."

Now, that gnawed at me for a long time, until one day I was teaching a Negotiations Training for Claims Adjusters class. I asked the question I usually ask at the beginning of the class, which is, "Does anybody have any questions before we get started?"

After the usual questions like, "What time is lunch?" and "When are we going to get out of here?" a young man raised his hand in the front of the room. He said, "Yes, I have a question for you. My boss took your class, this Negotiations class, a couple of months ago and he said that he really liked it. He said that in that class you had recommended a book, *You Could Negotiate Anything*, by a man named Cohen."

Needless to say I was impressed, but he wasn't finished yet. He continued, "I went out and bought the book and I have read through it. I highlighted some areas I had questions about and I would like to ask you those questions."

This individual's interest in wanting to learn made me realize that there really is a difference between people.

Although I respected my coworker's opinion, I realized that the system is important, but the difference between people is just as important. This person came to class with the desire and the expectation to learn something. He didn't come to class with the expectation that he was going to waste all day and just try to get through it. His attitude was, "I am going to be here and I am going to learn something."

It was the desire to learn, to want to do a good job, that gave him the edge that day. No one got as much out of that class as this individual because he came with the desire to learn something. Immediately I realized that the difference between average adjusters and good adjusters, or the difference

13

between good adjusters and outstanding adjusters, is not the talent of the individual in that particular job, it is something much more important.

This person who was in my class was not smarter than everyone else, not better educated than everyone else, nor a better negotiator than everyone else. He left, however, with a better degree of ability because of his desire to learn something. Then and there, I decided that I would be interested in identifying those qualities that make people outstanding adjusters.

As much as I believed in brain smarts, and GPAs, and college degrees, and technical skill and job knowledge as indicators of what to look for when selecting adjusters, all of my efforts to find the common elements that make truly great adjusters kept returning me to this conclusion.

That is, the very best adjusters, the best of the best, are linked not by intelligence, or educational background, or job knowledge. They are linked by certain characteristics that make them the best adjusters. I have found eight to be the most prevalent and most common among this elite group.

Although admittedly not a scientific approach, as I did not do any long-term research or analysis, I believe I have identified eight characteristics that truly make an adjuster one of the best: the Awesome Adjuster.

How did I identify these eight? Well, I started with Ann. Ann was a school counselor at the time, with a master's degree in Counseling/Psychology. I had been told by numerous people that she was considered the best counselor they had ever seen. She was, quite simply, awesome.

I asked people what made her the best, and I was surprised by their answers. Instead of getting answers such as "She knows all the rules," or "She has lots of experience," I got answers such as "She has a great attitude," "She's really a team player," and "She really tries to understand where people are coming from" (being married to her, I knew they were right).

When I thought about it, I realized that in claims, we are not too far removed

14

from being counselors. People are in need of help, and we are the ones who are supposed to help them. So I decided to start out with the things that make someone a great counselor, and see if they apply to the claims adjuster position. Turns out, those three did.

I came up with a few on my own, and I had it nailed down to seven characteristics. It seemed like there was something missing, however, that I just couldn't put my finger on. Then my daughter Amanda (child genius), said to me one day, "Some people in my school could be so smart if they only took some initiative and applied themselves."

There it was. The eighth characteristic that separates the Awesome Adjuster from the rest of the pack was initiative. I had my eight. Want the full list? Then keep reading.

CHAPTER 2

What is an Awesome Adjuster?

Let me take a moment to describe what I mean by an Awesome Adjuster.

Customers just love them because they are friendly and helpful.

Co-workers respect them for their knowledge and try to involve them in any particular project they are working on because they know that person will be a positive force.

Managers just love this person because they always seek ways to make things work, instead of finding ways that they won't. They question the status quo, without waging war against company policy.

The Awesome Adjuster is the top 5%, maybe 10% of all adjusters at a given company. They are the elite. They are the ones who will ultimately rise through an organization and will positively facilitate organizational change. The more observations and training I do, the more I am convinced that the individual skills are not what make up an Awesome Adjuster. It is the eight basic characteristics that I will outline in this book.

Can everyone learn to be an Awesome Adjuster? Of course not. That's not possible; they are only the top 5% - 10%. However, everyone can learn to be better than they were, even if it is just to work on one characteristic at a time. Everyone can take a new look at themselves to decide whether or not they truly want to improve, and what they are going to do to improve themselves. This book is a sort of guide. A road map, if you will, to help people better understand the changes they must make in order to become more productive, and of course more satisfied, workers.

GATHERING THE DATA

As mentioned in the Introduction section, I did not conduct formal research. I have no control groups to test out my theories, and no written documentation to substantiate each and every hypothesis. What I do offer is practical experience and examples to better qualify the eight characteristics of the Awesome Adjuster.

As a supervisor, manager, and regional manager, I had the opportunity to work with many adjusters from the entry level up through management. As a consultant, I had the opportunity to come into companies to flow-chart their work, interview adjusters, review training programs, and map out work processes. I was also responsible for making recommendations in training and adjuster development.

As President of International Insurance Institute, I am often called in to companies to monitor phone calls in order to develop training, and make recommendations.

Based on this extremely broad level of both adjuster and customer interaction, I have developed ideas about the eight characteristics of the Awesome Adjuster. I hope they prove worthwhile.

Before you move to the next chapter, I have a question for you. Did you find this book on your own? Are you reading it because the subject matter interests you, or did someone give this book to you to read?

For those of you who sought this information on your own, continue onto the next chapter. For those who were given this book, for whatever reason, I'd like to ask you to do something. I'd like you to jump forward to Chapter 6. Read that chapter, and if you are still interested, come back to Chapter 3. There is something that I think is important for you to know before you continue on reading this book.

CHAPTER 3

Attitude

The most important characteristic of the eight is attitude. However, many people misunderstand attitude, what it is, what it means, and how to alter it. Most adjusters, like most people in general, live their lives believing that attitude is a function of all the things that happened to them, rather than something that they can affect and change.

Let me ask you, the reader, to ponder a question. If I were to say to you, "Your attitude is probably one of the more important factors of your success in your career," would you agree or disagree?

Most people would agree, but now let me ask you another question. What have you done today, actively, to improve your attitude towards your responsibilities in your career, your job, your job satisfaction or anything at all? When I say actively, I mean what have you actually done today: if not today, last week: if not last week, last month? What have you actively done to try to create an improved, more positive attitude in yourself?

Most people, although they will agree attitude is one of the most important factors of their success in their career, don't actually do anything to change their attitude. Is attitude something that you can change? Is attitude something you can control? Well, you are going to have to answer that question, and I am going to have to give you some guidelines on what you can do to change your attitude.

I believe people have the ability to change their attitudes. The only problem is . . . they don't want to. Especially the ones with bad attitudes. Many people who have a poor attitude, like their attitude. They believe they are justified in their attitude, even if it is negative.

They believe they are entitled to be angry with the company, annoyed by their supervisors, frustrated with their lack of responsibilities, etc.

And maybe they are. Yet it doesn't hurt anyone except themselves. They will cling to this baggage with all their might because they believe they are entitled to it, that they have earned it.

So what's wrong with that?

When I lived in Franklin, Tennessee, I was in church listening to a sermon by our pastor, Randy Dunnavant, at Church of the Good Shepherd. Although I do not remember the exact focus of the sermon, I do remember one important part of it.

Randy was talking about holding grudges and how some people have the ability to hold onto a grudge for an extremely long time. During the sermon, he commented, "Holding a grudge does nothing to the other person. Holding a grudge has no effect whatsoever on the person that you are holding it against. Holding a grudge only has an effect on you. It reminds you of the pain that you went through in order to hold the grudge in the first place."

That was an important comment: it points out that grudges, just like attitudes, are something that we choose to have and, therefore, can choose to alter. But can you choose to have a good attitude? Well, that depends what you're looking for, which I will discuss in this chapter on attitude. However, please keep an open mind that perhaps attitude is something you can control more than you might have thought.

WHAT IS IT THAT YOU ARE LOOKING FOR?

Although it might be difficult in book form, I'd like to ask you to do something that I sometimes have my students do. Right now, while you are reading this book, when I tell you to look, I want you to stop reading this page and look around the room for anything that is blue. Anything at all that is blue, or any shade of blue. I would like to see how observant you are.

When you get to the end of this page, stop reading, look around the room, try to observe everything you can that is blue and then look back down at this book and turn the page.

LOOK FOR BLUE NOW . . . THEN TURN THE PAGE

Now, without looking up from your book, think of everything you just saw
. . . that was red. Do not take your eyes of this page. But stop for a moment,
before you continue on with the next paragraph and think of anything that
you can remember that you just saw that was red.

Did you find that difficult? Why? Was there any red at all in the room? Could
you remember it? Why not? You might think that I tricked you and you will
respond by saying, "Well, you told me to look for blue so of course I didn't
see red." And you will have underscored my very point.

The point is people see what they are looking for.

Human beings are pretty simple creatures. We see what we are looking for.
There might have been red all around you; there might have been red right
in front of you. Why didn't you see it? Because we often overlook what is
right in front of us, if we are looking for something else hard enough. That
is the point. I can get you to see blue, green, or red. I can get you to see tri-
angles, circles, or squares. All I have to do is tell you to look for it, and you
will see it. Even to the exclusion of what is right in front of you.

Have you ever known anybody with a bad attitude? These aren't bad people;
they are just seeing what they are looking for. They are not bad in any way,
but since they are looking for the bad in things, that is what they see.

You know the type of person I'm talking about. You say to this person, "Hey
it's sunny outside" and they'll respond, "No I don't want to go outside, I'll
just get sunburned!"

You say to this person, "Well, maybe it will rain then," and they'll respond,
"Oh, I just washed my car, dammit!"

You say to this person, "Hey, I am going to give you a big fat raise" and the
person will respond, "No . . . that's more taxes . . . I don't want it."

Is this a bad person? No, this person is just seeing what they are looking for and that is all. The funny thing is, it is what this person is looking for that will affect their success and their career more than any other skill, talent, or technique that they master.

Can it be changed? Yes, but we still need to do a little more homework. I need to tell you about what I call the Rochelle Roy Response.

THE ROCHELLE ROY RESPONSE

I would like to take a minute and tell you what happened one day to me and Rochelle Roy. Rochelle was an adjuster of mine when I was a claims manager. I considered her an outstanding adjuster. I really didn't know why, all I knew was that I could trust her and she would always do a good job.

One day I entered the break room and I saw Rochelle reading her Claims Law book. Just as I walked in, I heard somebody say, "Shelly, it's just not fair that Carl gives you all this extra work to do. He's always giving you extra projects, expecting you to make extra efforts, and it's just not fair. He should spread the work around, and not make you carry such a load. You should say something to him."

Of course, I was ready to spout out my righteous indignation by saying something along the lines of, "Well I am the manager here, and I can do whatever the heck I want to . . . " or whatever I was going to say. But before I could spit that out, Rochelle stopped reading, looked up at this person and said, "I know Carl gives me a lot of extra work to do. He must think highly of me and trust me quite a bit to do that. And when people think highly of me, I work hard not to let them down." Then she resumed reading her Claims Law book.

Of course, I resisted the urge to drop to my knees and cry out, "I'm not worthy, I'm not worthy," because that was a pretty good response. As a matter of fact, it was an outstanding response. Somehow, Rochelle recognized that all of the extra work I gave her was my outward expression that I believed in her

23

more than anybody else.

Somehow, Rochelle recognized that I must have trusted her highly or else I wouldn't have given her extra work. I wouldn't have placed my faith in her for all to see. Somehow, amongst all of the work, Rochelle could recognize this opportunity when she saw it.

The most obvious display of someone with a positive attitude is when that person can recognize opportunity when they see it. They say the trouble with opportunity is that it is disguised as hard work. And that's true, that's a big problem with opportunity.

Bear in mind, Rochelle was not someone who walked around the office, glad that she got five claims dumped on her on a Friday at 4:30 PM. She had her days when the work piled up, and she had her days when dealing with customers would get frustrating. But somehow, she recognized that the extra work she was being asked to do was an opportunity. Somewhere in all that work was an opportunity that no one else got, the opportunity to prove that she could do it when maybe no one else could.

How about that person who made the comment to Rochelle? Was she trying to help Rochelle, or bring her down? Probably bring her down. You know, there are people (and these are not bad people either), that honestly believe the only way they can succeed is to bring everyone else around them down. They are not trying to be mean; they simply have no idea of how to achieve without bringing other people down.

Rochelle saw that comment for what it was — an attempt to lower her attitude, and she would have nothing of it. She saw that my extra demands on her were my outward expression that I trusted and thought more of her than anyone else. She was not about to throw away a hard earned opportunity like that.

THE NON-ROCHELLE ROY RESPONSE

I must say that Rochelle's response was a whole lot better than my response about three weeks earlier. I was in my boss's office, and I was bitching, whining, and complaining like you wouldn't believe. I was saying things like, "The other managers wanted me to do this, and HR asked me to do that, and that took all day Saturday, and now I have to do this traveling," and blah blah blah.

I was complaining, bitching, whining, and crying for five, six, maybe seven minutes or so. I bitched and complained and bitched some more (I figured I was bound to get a company car out of this or something.) But the whole time I was complaining, my boss was just staring at me, waiting for me to finish.

Finally, after about six, seven minutes or so, I finally ran myself down and stopped. He looked at me for a few seconds and said, "Carl, are you finished?" And I said, "Yeah, I'm finished." And he said, "Good, because I want to remind you of something." And I said, "Yeah, what?"

He said, "Carl, you asked for this job, remember? You sat here . . . in this office . . . and went into detail about how tough this job was going to be and why you were the only person I should select. Carl, you practically begged me for this job. Twenty-two people applied for this job, Carl, and you got it. I saw something in you I didn't see in anybody else. Maybe I was right, and maybe I was wrong, but here's your chance to prove it either way."

Slumping down in my chair, I listened as he continued, "If you want an easy job, go to McDonald's. A little buzzer goes off when the fries have to come out. If that's what you want, no hard feelings. Go! But before you leave my office, Carl, let me remind you of something. You got something 21 other people didn't get. You got the chance to prove you could do this job. No one else even got the chance. So do what you want to do."

Now, this wasn't a "win one for the Gipper" speech, this was a "Get your ass out of my office because you begged me for this job," speech. And guess what? He was right! I did beg him for that job. I sat in his office for four hours interviewing for that promotion, telling him how tough it was going to be and how no one else could do it. Yet once I got the job, all I could see was the hard work. All I could see were the demands and the tough things I had to do. I knew it was a tough job, which was why I asked for it in the first place. I just couldn't see the opportunity anymore.

Somehow, my boss recognized that all of the extra hard work I was going to have to do was my opportunity to prove that he was right for hiring me in the first place. That all of that hard work was my opportunity to show I was the right person for the job. The hard work was the challenge that I wanted, and would produce satisfaction I would feel from knowing I could do a difficult job that not many people could do.

Somehow, Rochelle recognized that all of the extra work I was giving her was my outward expression that I believed in her, and the hard work was her opportunity to prove me right. Somehow, I was the only one in this mix not getting it.

Somehow, my attitude had gotten turned around and I found myself looking for the wrong things. It wasn't entirely my fault, I simply hadn't been trained. Trained in what? The key in knowing how to recognize opportunity when it is there. To show you what I mean, I must tell you the story of the "Acres of Diamonds."

ACRES OF DIAMONDS

"Acres of Diamonds" is a story written by Russell Conwell. I first heard about the Acres of Diamonds in a book called *The Psychology of Achievement* by Brian Tracy. Mr. Tracy does an outstanding job paraphrasing the story, and I will try to do the same.

"Acres of Diamonds" is a short story about an old African farmer at the turn of the century. He's doing quite well on his farm. However, one day he hears about people discovering diamond mines and becoming fabulously wealthy. So he sells his land, sells his tools, sells all of his animals and heads off into Africa in search of diamond mines.

Well, 12, 13, 15 years later, broke, destitute and alone, he throws himself into the ocean and drowns. Meanwhile back on his farm, the new farmer is watering down his donkey in a stream. He looks down and he sees a rock; a rock that reflects light in a remarkable way.

He picks up the rock and takes it into town, and someone who knew what it was says, "Well, this is a diamond." And the farmer says, "It doesn't look like a diamond."

The man replies, "Well no, it doesn't look like a diamond. You have to cut it, clean it, and shine it, but it's a diamond. Can you take me back to where you found it?" So the farmer took the man back to his farm.

They went back to the farmer's land, and the new farmer looked down on his land and saw another rock. He picked it up and saw that it also was a diamond. Then he saw another rock, and that was a diamond. Again, he found another rock, and that was a diamond. And lo and behold, he looks up, and he finds that he is literally standing on acres of diamonds.

Now the moral of the story isn't that you have to look under your own two feet. The moral of the story is, if you are going to look for something, you'd better know what it's going to look like when you find it. This goes back to the old saying that the trouble with opportunity is that it is disguised as hard work.

Most of us want opportunity. We want a job that's challenging and praise when it is done well. Unfortunately, we don't see that we have that very job simply because we don't know how to recognize it when we find it.

It is hard to imagine, but sometimes the challenges and opportunities you desire most may well be what you have in your hands. If so; you may be a little bit like Mike Rhoda.

THE RHODA SITUATION

As a claims manager, I once had an adjuster named Mike Rhoda. I considered Mike to be an excellent adjuster; intelligent, hardworking, and conscientious.

I remember Mike's wife coming up to me at a party one time saying, "Carl, I want my husband back. He's been a claims adjuster for 6 months and he doesn't believe anything anybody tells him anymore." I responded with, "Why, what happened?" She said, "We had friends over the other night. When they told us they had gone on a cruise, Mike asked them if they had photos to prove it."

Anyway, one day, Mike came up to me and we had the following conversation:

Rhoda: *You know Carl, being a claims adjuster is not what I want.*

Van: *What is it that you want?*

Rhoda: *I want a job where I have responsibility.*

Van: *Responsibility? You practically hold people's lives in your hands while you're handling their claim.*

Rhoda: *Well, I want a job where I have authority.*

Van: *Authority? You've got authority. You can write a ten thousand dollar check without blinking. How many of your friends can pay out ten thousand dollars of their company's money without needing someone else's approval?*

Rhoda: *Well, I want a job where I can help people.*

Van: *Help people? These people are in desperate need of help.*

Rhoda: *No, they just whine, and cry, and bitch.*

Van: *Well Mike . . . what do people do when they need help? What does a job like that look like?*

I've seen people leave claims because they simply did not recognize the very thing that they were seeking. Ordinary things. The first step in becoming an Awesome Adjuster is the desire to improve. From that point on, it is focusing on recognizing opportunities when they are there and being able to see them through all the hard work. It's not easy, but it's not impossible.

Most people have no idea how to change their attitude even if they want to. To give you an example of how hard it can be, and give you hope that if Bob can do it, anyone can, I will share the saga of Bob.

THE SAGA OF BOB

When I was a new manager, but before I had the opportunity to meet the people I would be managing, my predecessor took me aside and gave me the run-down on everyone I would be managing. During this briefing, he said something to me that I will never forget. He said, "Now, Good Ole Bob here, he is very knowledgeable. He's very technically sound; you just have to watch out because he has a bad attitude."

During the conversation, he went into detail about the bad attitude Bob displayed at meetings and around the office, and how many times in his past performance reviews Bob had been told that he needed to improve. I didn't think too much of it at the time until it hit home.

At our first office meeting, I found that this office had a particular routine.

Someone would bring up something new, some kind of change they would like to see, and then everyone would all wait for good ole Bob to say something nasty or negative about it. He would, of course, and then we would continue on talking about it to see if we couldn't work something out. It was like a little dance that we'd all do in giving Bob his opportunity to get it out and move on with business.

It didn't take me too long until I realized that this was a very negative influence. As a matter of fact, we showed Bob more respect, and gave him more time, than just about anybody else because we all knew it was coming. In order to ease the pain of it happening, we all just waited for it to happen and then continued on. The bad side of this was, often he would convert someone to his side with his negative thinking before anybody really got any time to consider what we were trying to do.

Not only that, but then I noticed that during the day, Bob would spend time in the break room, chatting with other people, always pushing off his negativism, which of course can be contagious. What the prior manager told me was true, Bob was an excellent technician. He did his job according to his job responsibilities very well. Unfortunately, I spent a lot of time trying to clean up issues that had been twisted around by Bob. It didn't take too long until I realized that I had to do something about this problem.

At first I thought, well, I can sit down with Bob and go through all the things he needs to change and how it will help him in his career if he does make a change in his attitude. Then I had a chance to read his past five performance reviews and realized that he's been told this for many, many years. In fact, he has admitted many times that he is always being told that he needs to change his attitude and he'll even agree that that was something he needed to do in order to get promoted. Yet he would never actually change anything.

Then I thought, well, maybe I should give him some extra responsibilities and have him be responsible for leading a project. Yes, that would work. Put him in charge of fixings the things he says need fixing. I thought this was a perfect idea until a manager friend of mine pointed out that all that would do was show everyone in the office that the way you get rewarded with extra responsibilities is to bitch and complain about everything. That will send exactly the wrong message.

So I really didn't know what I was going to do until one day I decided I couldn't take it anymore, and I decided to give myself a gift. I decided to give myself a present; I decided then and there that in 30 days I was not going to have this problem anymore. In 30 days, this issue would be over. Either I would fire Bob, or I would fix him, one of the two was absolutely going to happen in 30 days and after that date, I would not have this problem anymore.

Since I really didn't have any idea on how to fix Bob, I subconsciously decided that I was going to fire him. Being an ex-auditor, I knew that would be very easy to do. No matter how good someone's work was, I could always find something wrong and blow it up into a big deal. That's what auditors do. So this really wouldn't be a problem and I set my sights on this happening.

I knew it would take me the whole 30 days to do, and I hunkered down to organize my action plan. I was going to get rid of this piece of evil that was a barrier to office attitude Nirvana. This bad seed was going down, and I was convinced firing Bob was the only realistic option . . . until that night.

That night something amazing happened. I happened to be watching an episode of "All in the Family." Meathead and Gloria were going off to protest something at a state office or something like that. And this was clearly irritating Archie. Meathead and Archie were arguing about it for a few minutes when Archie finally says to Meathead, "Look, if you don't like this country why don't you just get the hell out!"

When I heard that, I jumped up and said, "Yeah, Bob, if you don't like it in my claims office and it's so bad, then why don't you get the hell out of my office!" And I was cheering Archie on. I was cheering him on until Meathead said something that absolutely blew me away. Meathead responds to Archie, "Archie, I love this country, that's why I complain when I see something wrong."

That comment floored me because I realized that Meathead wasn't complaining for complaining's sake, he was actually trying to change something. He was trying to change what was happening into something better. It hit me right then and there that people who complain and bitch and always point out the negative, may not be bad people.

They may honestly believe that in order to help, they must point out all of the pitfalls. To be a positive influence, they have to warn people of the things that could happen or why things may not work. They're trying to help us avoid all of the destruction if something doesn't work out. These might not be bad people; they are just seeing what they are looking for.

That evening I decided I wasn't going to give up on Bob just yet. I decided to give Bob the benefit of the doubt and to see what I could do to actually affect change. I reread his performance reviews and realized something astounding. Although every single manager Bob ever had pointed out in detail that he needed to change his attitude in order for him to avoid being fired and receive promotions, they left out the most important thing. They left out HOW he was supposed to change.

How would Bob go about changing his attitude? No one had given him any instruction or any training whatsoever on how to actually do this. I realized that for five years Bob had been asked to do something he had no training in and no instruction on, he was just told to do it. I decided I was going to help Bob make that change. Well at least for the next 29 days I'd help him. Now I was faced with the same problem everyone else had: how do I get Bob to change? I have found there's a key to getting people to change. Keep in mind, most people like their attitude. They cling to it. They believe that they deserve it and that they are entitled to it, so they don't want to let it go. We all know that the only way to get someone to change is that they have to want to change.

There's an old joke my mother once told me that goes like this (bear in mind

I didn't say it was a funny joke): How many psychiatrists does it take to change a light bulb? The answer is, it only takes one, but the light bulb has to really want to change.

I told you it wasn't funny. Nevertheless, it points out something important. The only way to get Bob to change is that he's got to want to change. Until he wanted to, it was pointless. So that became my number one focus. How will I get Bob to want to change?

Well, I could do what all the other managers in the past had done and threaten him with losing his job, and that would probably work for a short period of time until he had been removed from written warning long enough to go back to his old ways.

Or, I could hold out a carrot in front of him and offer promotions and big raises if he changed his attitude, which never worked before either. Somehow I was going to have to come up with something different. And I really didn't know what that was going to be until I read a fascinating article about a restaurant that changed the answer to the most infamous question in dining history: "Save room for dessert?"

SAVE ROOM FOR DESSERT?

The article was written about a restaurant that had a very high percentage of people ordering dessert after their meals. As everyone knows, the percentage of people ordering dessert after a meal is very low. About 10% would be a good guess. After you have had a nice big meal and the waiter comes over to you and says, "Did you save room for dessert?" Your response probably is, "No." But this restaurant had a very high percentage of people ordering dessert, something around 80% if I can remember correctly. What was it that this restaurant did that all the other restaurants didn't do?

My first thought was, maybe they just didn't feed their customers very much. Maybe the initial portions were really small and they were still hungry. But it turned out that that wasn't the case; their portions were just as big as other restaurants'.

The article mentioned that normally a waiter will come over and ask, "Did you save room for dessert?" and most people's response is, "No." Only 10% will say yes. But if a restaurant wants to increase the chance of you ordering dessert, what might they do? One thing they could do is come over and describe the dessert, and that has a positive effect. It has a positive effect because having imagined that there was some mystery dessert out there, you now have the ability to focus on one, such as chocolate mousse or cheesecake. And the better the description of how it is made, and prepared, and served, the more appetizing it becomes, because now the person has to rely less on their imagination. This process does work very well and does increase people ordering dessert a couple of percentage points, maybe to 14% or 15%.

Another thing a restaurant could do is to give you a list that describes the desserts. That works well too because now you are actually reading them and getting images in your mind as you are reading them. And this makes you have a connection between the dessert itself and the enjoyment you will receive. This is even more effective than just describing it; however it still relies on your imagining the reward. But, it does push the percentage up to a good 19% or 20%.

Another thing a restaurant can do is to show you a picture of the desserts. This works very well in increasing the percentage another few points. Now there is a stronger connection between the description and what it would taste like. The reward becomes more real, but once again it is only a few more percentage points effective, because it still relies on the person imagining what it would taste like and the pleasure that they will receive. Let's guess it goes up to 23% or 24%.

In some restaurants (and you know which ones they are), they actually come around with a tray of desserts and point them out to you, describing each one in detail and using all of the techniques that all the other restaurants used except they put that dessert right in front of you. And this works best of all.

This also brings it up a few more percentage points, maybe 25%, heck maybe 30%. Those who have it right in front of their face will order dessert, because it strengthens the bond between imagination and enjoyment. Unfortunately, it still relies on that old tool of getting you to imagine how much you will enjoy it in order to get you motivated to buy it.

Well, 25% to 30% is much better than 10%, but remember now, this restaurant I had read about had 80%. How? Simple. They did not rely on what I call the "Imagine This" motivational technique.

Getting people to imagine their reward, or to imagine their pain, in order to motivate them is very ineffective. Even though we have good imaginations, it is still not real to us.

Take two different people and tell one person to imagine what they would do if they did not have a job right now. Ask them to imagine they were immediately fired, right this moment, and watch them calmly go through describing the opportunities and the choices they would have, and how they would respond.

Now, take the other individual and tell them that they are actually fired, and watch the sheer panic go through them. They're not just imagining it, they are actually experiencing it. Watch them change into another person as the reality of everything that will happen hits them. Watch them become motivated to do whatever it takes to stop this from happening. Or, even if they didn't like their job and were considering leaving it anyway but just never had the time to update their resumé, watch how motivated they become now to go look for a better job.

In my opinion, this is management's greatest failure in the United States: the practice of getting people to imagine either their rewards or their penalties before they have experienced it. How will you ever motivate someone by trying to get them to imagine their reward, before they have experienced it? This is the only tool we have of course, so we use it even though it is not very effective.

I was about to use this same, ineffective tool myself with good ole Bob, until I read this article about a restaurant, and it changed my mind about the limited tools we have at our disposal.

This restaurant did something much more effective than asking someone to use the "Imagine This" technique. They didn't just bring out the dessert; they brought out a tray of only one tiny bite of each of their desserts. Instead of asking customers if they wanted to try it, they simply walked up with the tray, bent down, put the tray in front of the customer and said, "Which one would you like to try?"

Now you, and I, and everyone who reads this book, all know that no matter how full we are, we can always handle one little piece of cheesecake. There's always room for a little tiny piece of chocolate torte, no matter how full we are.

Guess what would happen? Virtually every customer would try at least one little bite. And then, something amazing would happen, they tasted it. It was real; it wasn't imaginary anymore. They would actually taste it; it was in their mouth and it tasted good. They liked it. What this restaurant found was that there was a very high percentage of people that would now order dessert. It also found that virtually everyone who ordered a dessert, ordered the very thing that they tasted. That's the way the restaurant knew that there was a high correlation between what people tasted, and what they ordered.

This was a real motivational force and I decided to use it. If a restaurant could get people to order dessert when they are not hungry simply because they can make that taste real for them, maybe I could do this for Bob. I still had a few big problems though.

The first one was I had to get Bob to want to change; the second thing was I had to teach him how. I outlined what I needed to do, and I came up with this:

STRATEGY TO GET BOB TO CHANGE:

1. Get him to want to change.
> Find out what he desires.
> Set an expectation that he can achieve his desires.
> Give him a taste.

2. Teach him how to change.
> Change what he is looking for.

I called Bob into my office and had him sit down. Of course he was a little nervous because most people don't get called into the boss's office unless they are in trouble, but he was relatively calm anyway.

I sat down on the same side of the desk with Bob and I started to talk to him. I wanted to find out the types of things that he wanted and what motivated him. This information didn't come easy, but after that 20, maybe 30 minutes or so I found out something very interesting about Bob. Bob was not a bad person. He was absolutely just seeing what he was looking for. He had no way to look for the positive, all he knew how to do was look for the negative.

I found out that what Bob wanted was what everybody wanted. He wanted to be respected for his knowledge, be revered for his ability to do his job; he wanted to be seen as an authority figure in the office, someone people would come to for advice. I saw very little difference in Bob than most of my adjusters.

However, there is an old saying that goes like this:
> *There is very little difference between people, but that little difference can make a big difference. The little difference is attitude, and the big difference is whether it is positive or negative.*

I now had some advantages that perhaps the previous managers did not have. I now knew that I had to get Bob to want to change, and that I had to give him a taste of what it would be like if he did. I also had to teach him how to do it. I had to give him a process that he could follow. In short, I had to train

Bob by giving him a little taste of reality.

THE TASTE OF REALITY

As sneaky as it might be, this was my approach. About a week after the discussion where I found out about Bob's desire to be respected and valued, I called Bob into my office and once again we had an informal chat. When I felt the time was right, and Bob was somewhat at ease, I said the following to Bob:

"Bob, I just want to thank you and congratulate you for everything you have done. I asked you to make a change in your attitude, and you've done a remarkable job. You have absolutely been a positive influence in the office, and it is returning some great results. People are coming to me now and saying how they were so surprised that you really did know so much and that they wanted you on their teams for their projects. People respect you and they clearly understand how much you really do know. You've made my job easier by being a positive influence in the office and I want to congratulate you on it. I want to admit to you that many people didn't think you could do it. Many, many people thought that you would never change and you've proven them wrong. You've risen above everybody's expectations. Great job."

Now after I said this to him, he looked rather puzzled, because he himself knew that he didn't make any change at all. That was okay for the time being. I then asked him an important question. I said to Bob, "Well, Bob, how does it feel to get all that feedback?" And Bob said, "Good. It feels good, no one has ever said that to me before, it feels really good." And then I said to Bob, "Well, that's good, because that's the feedback I am going to give you when you make the change in your attitude. That's what I'm going to tell you when you change your attitude for the positive, like I've asked you to do. If you like that taste, there is much more coming."

Now you, the reader, might feel that I tricked Bob, and in a way I admit I did. I suppose it was a little sneaky but I gave Bob a taste. Even though he knew he didn't deserve it, he got a taste of something he had never been given before. He needed that positive feedback that he was succeeding in the office. And guess what? He liked it! In fact, he wanted more. And I could see those thoughts running through his mind about how good that tasted and how badly he wanted some more.

He then asked me a question; it was the most important question on his road to recovery. He turned to me and asked, "What do I have to do?"

Right then I knew I had something. I'd given Bob a taste of what he wanted and I got something in return. What I got was a clear indication that Bob wanted to change. He now wanted to change because he had tasted something he liked and he wanted more. I knew right then and there I had achieved my first objective with Bob. And now came the easy part. Now, all I had to do was teach him how he could change.

LOOK FOR WHAT YOU WANT TO SEE

My personal motto was: you will see what you are looking for, therefore look for what you hope to see. I tried to put this into play with Bob. What I said to Bob was, "Bob, here's what I want you to do. The next time we are in an office meeting and someone says something about any type of change, what will happen?" Bob responded, "I will find something bad about it." "Right," I said, "So here's what I want you to do. When somebody says something is going to happen, instead of that thing happening, I want you to imagine that the opposite happened. I want you to imagine that whatever circumstance someone mentions, or whatever project is brought up, or whatever event that happened, I want you to do the best you can to imagine that the opposite happened. Then, when you automatically think of the negative of that alternate event, then the opposite of that negative will be the positive of the real event."

Bob was looking at me kind of like you are probably looking at this book right now, with a big puzzled look on your face trying to make sense of what I just said. But I have to hand it to Bob; he did his best. At the next office meeting we were informed that we were closing down a claims office near us, and all of that office's work was coming to us. Every bit of work was now going to be handed down to us with the same amount of staff that we currently had. Yes, we would gradually be able to increase our staff, but in the meantime we would all have to handle the extra work. As soon as that announcement was made, everybody (including me), stopped and looked down at the end of the table at Bob. We are all thinking, "This is going to be a good one."

Bob sat there, and before he could say anything, I saw him trying to do what I asked him to do. He sat there with this head bobbing up and down like one of those little dogs in the back of a car window, trying to think of what it was I had asked him to do. And after about 10 seconds, Bob finally spit it out. And what came out was, "Well, at least it's job security!"

Everybody in the office meeting was stunned. We turned our heads, looked at Bob and we were all thinking, "WHAT? That came out of Bob?" Nobody could believe it; Bob had something positive to say and no one knew how it happened. What Bob did was exactly what I asked him to do. (See Figure 3.1)

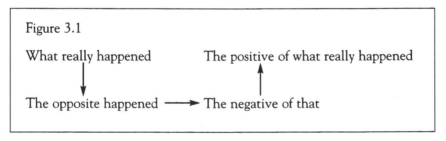

Figure 3.1

What really happened   The positive of what really happened

The opposite happened ——→ The negative of that

What I asked Bob to do was for anything that came up, to think of the opposite. So when we were told that the other office was shutting down and the work was coming to us, what does that mean? The real event is that we are going to have to do a lot more work. What I asked Bob to do was imagine the opposite of that event. The opposite of more work is less work. (See Figure 3.2)

Then I asked Bob to come up with the immediate negative of that alternate event. What is the negative of having less work? Well, layoffs.

Once Bob thought of layoffs, I asked him for one more step. I told him that whatever negative he thought of that came out of the alternate event, the opposite of that would be the positive of the real event. And what is the opposite of layoffs? Job security.

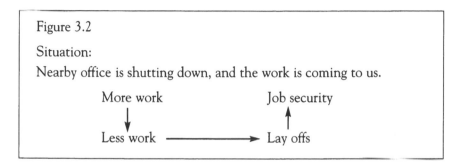

Figure 3.2

Situation:

Nearby office is shutting down, and the work is coming to us.

It took him a while, it took a couple seconds of his head bobbing up and down, but he somehow got from more work coming into the office to job security. It didn't come easy, but at least he had a process to follow now that he didn't have before.

The first time it took Bob maybe 10 seconds with saliva coming out as he blurted out "job security." Soon he stopped slobbering, and after a week or two, he didn't even have to bob his head anymore. He could get from the event happening, to the positive in it, in a matter of a couple of seconds. And after a few weeks, it hardly seemed like work for him anymore. He was now able to recognize that there were positives in any event. Instead of looking for ways things wouldn't work, he was able to say why they could and how to make them work.

I'm happy to say that today Bob is a successful manager. The only thing he needed was training on how to have a positive attitude. No one had ever given this to him before. I was pleased to be able to affect even a small change. I look back on it now and think I was just a few days away from firing him. Bob was not a bad person; he just needed training.

Now that we worked through that one, I want to propose another scenario. Another diamond in the rough was a person that we used to call Mother Teresa.

MOTHER TERESA, THE COMPLAINT MAGNET

Teresa had only been working for me for a few months. She had transferred in from a different area in the company, and I greatly respected her skills and knowledge. She was an excellent technician and was very dedicated to her work. I noticed Teresa started to work longer hours as the months went by and, at the same time, I started seeing a change in her attitude. She was more discouraged in office meetings and less willing to accept change.

When I tried to talk to Teresa about it, she would always bring up things that were happening to other people. She would tell me how John lost his benefits, because he wasn't working enough hours, and how mad she was at the company for that. She would tell me how Susan didn't get the promotion just because she had a cross word with her manager, etc. After a few minutes listening to this, I realized that almost everything that was turning her attitude sour had nothing to do with her. When I asked her to focus on what was going on with her, she started saying that she was a little disgruntled, because she had been working long hours, but then she went right back to describing the woes of other people.

Over the next few days, I noticed something fascinating, something I hadn't ever noticed before. What I noticed was that people were going into Teresa's office all during the day, sitting down, and talking with her. Of course, previously I thought that they were seeking her advice, because she was very knowledgeable. But then I noticed that the people she was talking to, tended to be the very people she voiced concerns about. She was voicing their concerns.

People liked to come in and talk to her and tell her all their woes for a very simple reason: she would listen. She would offer some advice, but mainly she offered consolation. Therefore, the more consolation she offered, the more people would come to her. Then, once they found out that she had actually voiced their concerns to management, as she did to me, well then she would get flooded with more people coming to her, so she could be the champion for their cause. Teresa was a complaint magnet.

I found out that she was even lovingly referred to as "Mother Teresa" in our office. Presumably named after *the* Mother Teresa.

I went to Teresa and talked to her about this and how it was having a negative affect on her, which of course she rejected as ridiculous. One thing I learned about Teresa was that she liked it. She liked people seeing her as the person they could come to, that she would be their savior. As a result, she was working a couple of extra hours every day to support this activity, and now it was having a negative affect on her attitude.

I needed to do something with Teresa, but I wasn't quite sure what; then I decided to see if I could apply my formula for changing a person. I remembered the keys were knowing what a person wants, showing them that what they want can be achieved and then giving them a taste.

With Teresa, it was no problem knowing what she wanted. In the few months I had been working with her, it was obvious she wanted to leave work on time. Working extra hours was shrinking the time she could spend with her children at home. This was very important to her. So knowing what she desired came without any work at all. Figuring out how to give her a taste of that, well that was not going to be so easy. You see, Teresa rejected the notion that her consultations took very long. She was convinced this was just a few minutes a day.

Then, it hit me. I would give her a vacation. That's right; I would give her a paid vacation!

That next day I called Teresa into my office and I said, "Teresa, I'm going to give you a paid vacation." She looked at me rather puzzled, and then I continued on by saying, "Not out of the office, but a paid vacation from people bringing their problems to you. For one week, I'm going to pay you for just your job, and no one is going to be allowed to come into your office to complain about anything. If someone does go into your office, I will stand there and make sure you only talk about work. But for one week you are going to have no one in your office to complain about anything, you are only going to do your job."

Teresa tried to come up with every excuse on why that would not work but finally agreed after a while. Later that day in the office meeting I made my announcement that Teresa, for one week, was not allowed to talk to anybody else unless it was strictly about work, and I would be there in the office to make sure. I didn't explain why, I simply said that Teresa is going on a week's vacation from anybody going to her with their problems.

At first people kind of rolled their eyes and thought Carl was out of his head again, but I decided to see it through. Sure enough, Monday morning, it wasn't one hour after work started that I saw someone in Teresa's office. I walked in and heard the tail end of their conversation which clearly wasn't anything about work. Both the person and Teresa tried to pretend it was something about work but when they couldn't fake it, that person just left. This went on for the first day and everybody kind of laughed and saw it as a big game.

On the second day, people actually did stay away and I didn't have to chase them out anymore. I then noticed something: Teresa was pretty much focusing on her work. By Wednesday, people weren't coming to her at all anymore. I realized then that previously, no one had come to her for advice on anything that had to do with work. Her time was being constantly consumed by people who wanted to complain about something. I noticed something else by Wednesday: Teresa actually left the office about an hour earlier than she used to.

She had been working until 7:00 PM almost consistently and now left about 6:00 PM. By Thursday she left about 5:30 PM. By Friday at the day's end I noticed that her desk was pretty much cleaned up and all but a couple items on her to-do list were left. She came into my office and closed the door and she asked something that made me smile.

She leaned over to my desk and very quietly whispered, "Carl, can I have another week's vacation?"

Once again, I had something. I knew that Teresa wanted to be home with her family and one of the reasons she was feeling disgruntled was because she didn't have enough time to pick up her kids from daycare and that made her sad. Very sad in fact, and she didn't like it. I knew what she wanted without her having to tell me; she wanted to be able to leave work on time. But I also knew that she liked being seen as Mother Teresa in the office. I knew that in order for her to want to leave on time badly enough to make a change, she needed a taste of what it would be like. She needed a taste, and I gave it to her. It was only a week, but it was good enough. She tasted it, she liked it, and she wanted more. By asking me if she could have another week's vacation, I knew what she was really asking me. She was really asking, "What do I have to do?"

My response was very simple,

Teresa, you can have as many weeks' vacation as you want. All you have to do is realize that every time someone comes to you to talk about their issues, what they are really saying to you is: Teresa, no matter what you have to do, no matter how important your kids are, it's not as important as the fact that I want to complain about something to you. Then Teresa, all you have to do is make a choice. Is it more important to you to be seen as Mother Teresa? Or is it more important for you to be home with your kids? I'll let you make that choice. If you are concerned about being rude, remember, the person who is interrupting you and making you work longer hours is the one who is really being rude. All you have to do is say, 'I'm sorry, I want to talk to you. Can we talk at lunch or at a break because right now I really need to get these things done?' If people can't respect that, then they are not your friends or people you need to worry about being rude to anyway.

I had Teresa wanting to change. She had a desire to leave work on time. She now had a reasonable expectation that that desire was achievable. And she had a taste of it.

By telling her what she had to do to get it, namely tell people to leave her alone, I taught her how to change. The rest was up to her. And guess what? She changed.
Once in a while, Teresa did slip back into her old ways, but then quickly rebounded once she realized she was working longer hours.

In these cases of Good Ole' Bob and Mother Teresa, it was a matter of people having to change their attitude, but not being given the training on how to do that. These are two very simple cases and certainly the steps taken by Bob and Teresa would not be the ones to take in every situation. It does, however, demonstrate that in order to make a change, a person has to both want to, and know how to.

My advice to anyone who wants success in claims is to start by working on their claims attitude. To do that, you must stop looking at all the work, and start looking for the opportunity. I suggest by beginning with the steps I used for Good Ole Bob:

> Decide what you want, what is important to you.
> Make sure it is something you can reasonably achieve.
> Give yourself a taste.

To be sure, giving yourself a taste is the hard part. To be really motivated to do anything, you have to stay away from the "Imagine This" technique, and give yourself a taste. Many self-help authors suggest simply pretending and acting as if you already have achieved what you want. The more you can pretend you have what you want, the more your attitude (and your actions) will be tailored to fit with it.

Another great technique is to practice rephrasing the things you say and hear in order to find some positive in it. Below are some comments I have

46

heard claims people make just during the last year or so. See if any of them sound familiar.

I have too much work.

My manager gives me all the difficult files.

Customers are always complaining.

If this job was easier, I'd like it better.

No one helps me unless I ask for it.

My job is nerve-racking. One little mistake could cost the company thousands.

The only time I see my supervisor is when I make a mistake.

I always have to go to conferences and review them for everyone else in office meetings.

The insureds are so needy. I wish they'd leave me alone.

I'm the only one in my office with any experience.

Here is the exercise. See if you can reword the comments to point out the positive. Keep in mind all of the comments are completely valid. But if you can change them around just a little so they seem positive instead of negative, you are ahead of the game.

In Figure 3.3 I have rewritten the comments as I believe an Awesome Adjuster would have seen things.

Figure 3.3

I have too much work.
> I have job security.

My manager gives me all the difficult files.
> My manager trusts me to handle the difficult files.

Customers are always complaining.
> Customers need my help. That's my job.

If this job was easier, I'd like it better.
> If this job was easier, the company wouldn't need me.

No one helps me unless I ask for it.
> I'm left alone to do my job.

My job is nerve-racking. One little mistake could cost the company thousands.
> I have a job that is important and requires thoughtful care. My company trusts my decisions.

The only time I see my supervisor is when I make a mistake.
> My supervisor doesn't hover over me and lets me do my job.

I always have to go to conferences and review them for everyone else in office meetings.
> I am trusted to interpret important information and help train others in my office.

The insureds are so needy. I wish they'd leave me alone.
> The insureds are very needy. If they weren't, anyone could do this job.

I'm the only one in my office with any experience.
> I am relied upon in my office because of my experience.

Spend just one week pretending you already have what you want, and rewording every negative comment you say or hear, and you will see an immediate change in your attitude toward your responsibilities. Your job satisfaction will go up, and your stress level will go down. Then, if you like the way that tastes, go ahead and indulge. Keep eating up that positive attitude. Don't worry; positive attitude is the ultimate diet. No fat and no carbs!

CHAPTER 4

Time Management

HOW DO I RETURN 50 PHONE CALLS A DAY?: THE WRONG QUESTION

One of the most important things to understand about effective time management is that, for most claims people, there is no way to get all of our work done. When I teach our Real-Life Time Management for the Claims Adjuster class, invariably someone will ask me this question: "How can I possibly return 50 phone calls in a day?" Usually when someone asks me that question my response is, "Well, I now know what your problem is. I can now help you. Because you asked me that question, I now know what you have been doing wrong." Of course they get a puzzled look, but then I continue.

Before I tell them the error of their ways, I usually recap a case study I had heard about. I have no idea what airline it was, but I had heard about an airline back in the 80s that had a terrible reputation in the Lost Luggage department. They decided one day that their reputation was so bad, that they were going to put one of their top executives in charge of the Lost Luggage department.

The first thing he did was bring his team together, all of his managers and superiors, and tell them that they had to improve, and they had to do it quickly. He asked for their ideas and solicited their advice. He had meetings once a week to implement ideas.

A funny thing happened: they improved. They did put in place the ideas from the people who were doing the job at the time, and it had a positive effect. After about six months, sure enough, they had greatly improved. They weren't number one, but they were sure a darned good Lost Luggage department.

They got together and they decided, "Well you know what? We want to be number one. We are not the best yet, but we can be." So they got back together, made a bunch of decisions with new ideas and implemented them as soon as they possibly could. And after about a year, they were number one. Yes, they were easily the best Lost Luggage department of any airline.

If you lost your luggage, you wanted to be on this airline for sure. They were doing things like putting pagers on luggage, and delivering flowers with bags, and just about everything else you could think of. They were absolutely number one. Yup, the best Lost Luggage department in the industry.

That year, they got back together and said, "Well, we want to be better than number one. We're the best, but we want to be better!" So they decided that because they had run out of ideas, they should hire a consultant.

Now personally as a consultant, I can tell you when you are on the outside looking in, it is very easy to see problems. When you are in the inside, it is not so easy to see. But, coming from the outside, they stare you right in the face.

So the consultant came in and they showed him all the processes, and they showed him everything that they had done, and they said, "Look! What can we do to be even better than number one? We want to be the very best Lost Luggage department that there ever was. What can we do?"

The consultant took a look around, saw what they did, turned to one of the top managers and said, "Well, why don't you just stop losing the luggage?"

As simple as it is, this is a true story; at least I heard that it's true. It is very, very common that a company will spend lots of time and lots of money running around trying to effectively react to a problem that they themselves created, instead of spending any time at all trying to not cause the problem in the first place. I have many real life examples of my own where, as a consultant, I have been asked to come up with a way to efficiently manage a problem, and the company never asked me to solve the problem in the first place. This is very common.

Let's get back to that claims question. When the person asked, "How can I return 50 phone calls in a day?," and my response was, "Well, now I know what your problem is." I would then continue on and say, "You see, you asked me the wrong question. The question isn't, 'How can I return 50 phone calls in a day.' That's the wrong question. The question is, 'What am I doing in the process that's making me get 50 phone calls?'" See, because if we can solve that problem, well then we don't have to worry about how to efficiently return 50 phone calls.

Most claims people trying to improve time management will look for ways to organize themselves and effectively handle more work, when usually that's not the issue. The issue is, "What am I doing that's causing more work? What can I do to eliminate those things that cause me more work, and how can I effectively prioritize the things that are left?"

Let's start with a very basic tool that can often cause less work.

WENDELL LAMBERT EFFECT

For those of you who might be in an environment where you have voice mail, let me ask you a question, and be honest with yourself. Have you ever been at your desk when the phone rings, and even though you're there, you don't pick it up? You let it roll into voice mail for several reasons. One might be you're working on something and you don't want to be interrupted. Another might be you don't want to deal with that person right now. There are lots of reasons, all justifiable.

To make a decision not to answer a call and let it roll into voice mail may be the right decision, it may be the wrong one, but it has to be viewed from the time management perspective. Remember, if you're doing something that causes you more work, then you're not being as effective as you can be.

If you have a choice of answering the phone or continuing on doing what you're doing so you won't be interrupted, then you have to ask yourself, "Which one of these is causing me more work?" If one of them is causing more work for you, then it becomes a priority to eliminate that extra work. So let's see how this plays out.

In Figure 4.1, there are two columns. Let's say you receive a hundred phone calls in a week that you could have answered, but you let roll into voice mail. Most adjusters receive far more than 100 calls a week, but let's just talk about the ones you let roll into voice mail that you could have answered.

In column one, let's say that you had the opportunity to answer all 100 of those phone calls. Of course, realize that this is not always possible because sometimes you're on the phone and the calls roll into voice mail, or sometimes you're not there. But let's just say for the sake of the argument, that these were calls you could have answered but didn't. And let's say that you do answer every single phone call. What's your total number of phone calls? 100, because you answered them all.

Now, look at column two. Let's say in the second scenario, instead of answering them, you let all 100 calls roll into voice mail. Now what do you have to do? You have to pick up 100 voice mail messages and write them down. Now what do you have to do with those 100 voice mail messages? Do you have to return all of those calls? Well, the answer is no.

Probably only about 90% you will actually have to call back, the other 10% will just be informational. So if you got 100 initially, about how many calls do you have to return? Right, you have to now make 90 outgoing calls after listening to a 100 voice mail messages. Keep in mind, just the task of writing down the message is already extra work because it went into voice mail. From the very beginning, you are now creating extra work for yourself.

Let me ask you the next question, do you actually get all of these 90 people on the phone? No, you'll get about half of them. So you'll talk to 45 and what do you do with the other 45 that you don't get? You'll leave a message for them of course. What do those 45 people do when they get this message that you've called? That's right, they call you back. Do all of them call you back? No, only about 90% will call back, because the other 10% might be informational that you could have just left in a message.

So let's say about 40 actually call you back. What happens when those people call you back? They roll into voice mail of course. Now what do you have to do? You have to pick up 40 voice mail messages and return phone calls. Do you have to return all of them? No, you only have to return about 90%, so you'll now make about 36 outgoing phone calls.

Do you get all of those people? No of course not, you only get about half, so you'll talk to 18 and guess what you do with the other 18? That's right, you leave a voice message for them. What do those 18 people do when they get those messages? That's right, they call you back. Not all of them, probably only about 90%, so maybe 15 or 16 call you back.

What do you do with those 15 phone calls when they come in? Well you let them roll into voice mail, and it goes on and on and on.'

Figure 4.1

100 Calls get answered   100 Calls go into voice mail

Total Calls – 100   100 – Pick up voice mail
                                90 – Return calls (leave 45 messages)
                                40 – Incoming calls into voice mail
                                36 – Return calls (leave 18 messages)
                                15 – Incoming calls into voice mail
                                13 – Return calls (leave 6 messages)
                                5 – Incoming calls into voice mail
                                4 – Return calls (leave 2 messages)
                                2 – Incoming calls into voice mail
                                1 – Return call (leave 1 message)
                                1 – Incoming call into voice mail
                                1 – Return call. All calls completed

                                _____

                                308 Total Calls

The general rule of thumb is that for every call you don't answer and you let roll into voice mail, you are quite literally generating three to four more phone calls later, either incoming or outgoing. The purpose of this exercise is to demonstrate that by not answering a call when you could, when it comes in, you actually generate more work for yourself later. You are causing yourself more work to do!

Now you're doing this for a very important reason: the reason is that you don't want to be interrupted. Unfortunately, the price you're paying for it is to create more work which will interrupt you more often later.

The key isn't just to allow yourself to be interrupted. The key is to figure out how to stop it from feeling like interruption. What if you could answer that phone call, deal with it, and get right back to what you were doing without it feeling like an interruption? Then you could handle both issues at the same time, and make the most effective use of your time. Can this be done easily? Well, it's not easy, but it's not impossible. Just ask Wendell.

Wendell Lambert comes from the Latin words Wendelis Lamberdicious, meaning "Answer Your Damn Phone." Actually, Wendell is a claims executive, who, for some strange reason, answers his phone. I commented to him one day that it was always a pleasure calling him, because he always answers his phone, and I never have to play telephone tag with him all the time. His response was, "I don't like wasting time, so I answer my phone."

So how can you answer your phone without it feeling like an interruption if you are working on something? This is where good To-Do list structure comes in. Most people do not like To-Do lists because they can never get around to getting anything on them finished. They keep getting interrupted, and it becomes frustrating.

What if you knew everything that was going to happen to you at the beginning of the day? Imagine that. Everything that you would eventually put on your To-Do list, you knew at the beginning of the day. Would that be a relief? Sure, because then you could prioritize everything you had and nothing would interrupt you.

Well, if that would make it easier, then treat the new things that come in during the day as if you already knew about them at the beginning of the day. Let's say you list out everything you need to do today (say you have 20 items), and something new comes in. Right now, you may be working on item #2, when you receive a message to call Joe Vendor. Simply add to your To-Do list "Call Joe Vendor," and rank it where you would have put it at the beginning of the day had you known about it. If you would have ranked it between #6 and #7, then put #6B next to it, and go back to working on item #2.

Let's say you finish item #2, and you begin working on item #3. Before you finish, you receive a note from your supervisor to review a file and write a summary for him by the end of the day. Then write on your To-Do list, "Review file and summarize," and simply decide where you would have put it had you known about it at the beginning of the day. If you would have put it between #5 and # 6, then mark it #5B. If you would have put it between #9 and #10, then mark it #9B. Then go right back to working on #3. If you do this throughout the day, these things coming in won't seem like such an interruption, and neither will answering your phone.

The point is, if knowing everything that is going to happen to you at the beginning of the day would help you, and cause you to feel less frustrated and interrupted, then treat it that way.

There are many great Time Management books with excellent suggestions on keeping proper To-Do lists. I highly recommend *Time Management* by Kevin Quinley. Right now, I'd like to focus on the thing that most adjusters say would make their jobs easier, and talk about the technique that can help.

IF CUSTOMERS WOULD JUST LISTEN

When I teach our Awesome Claims Customer Service classes, I always start off with an exercise. Please finish this sentence: "My job would be much easier if the customers would just _____." See fig 4.2. Please take a few moments and write out the answers.

Figure 4.2
Easier Job Exercise

Please complete the following sentence:
My job as an adjuster would be so much easier if the customers would just

_____.

Answers:

_____

_____

_____

_____

_____

_____

The response I almost always get is, LISTEN! That's right; my job would be so much easier if the customers would just listen. And of course what goes along with that is, "Remember what I just said."

I know some of you put things like, "Go Away," "Stop Calling," "Stop having accidents." Those are just fine. Sometime we have to blow off a little steam first. That's fine. Most of us claims people understand that if customers did go away and really did stop having accidents, we wouldn't have jobs. I even had someone say to me once, "If it wasn't for these damn customers, I'd get all my work done." I'm not sure what work that adjuster would have without customers, but I let the comment slide.

After the "blowing off steam" answers, you might have put answers like: "Cooperate;" "Do what I tell them;" "Listen;" "Remember what I say;" "Call less often;" "Be patient, and let me do my job."

So do you have any effect over these things? If you are thinking that you don't, I have some good news for you. As an adjuster, you have incredible power over things you never thought possible. All you need is a little training.

Can you affect whether customers listen to you?
Extremely.
Do you have influence over whether customers remember what you say?
Definitely.
Can you change customers' attitudes so that they will be more cooperative?
Absolutely.
Can you reduce the number of calls customers make to you? Unquestionably.

Let's take them one at a time.

INFLUENCING CUSTOMER LISTENING AND RETENTION

As an adjuster, you know there are plenty of times where you go through a nice big explanation of what's going to happen, and tell the customer everything they need to know.

And what happens right after you've finished the big long explanation? They ask questions of course, usually about what? Usually about what you just said. So what do you do? Well, you answer them. And what do they do? They ask more questions. And what do you do? You answer them. And now you're playing ping-pong, and you're sitting there, thinking to yourself, "Why don't they just listen?"

Do you have a way to affect whether or not people are listening to you? Do you have a way to affect whether or not people remember what you say? If you're still thinking to yourself no, then I have some very good news for you. You are absolutely going to learn a technique which will drastically improve when people are listening to you as well as remembering what you said when you're finished.

Having been a claims adjuster for six years, it's easy for me to come up with examples of when we tend to give people a lot of information. While you're reading this book, I want you to imagine times when you give, either your customers or maybe even your coworkers, a lot of information, and see if you don't fall into this same trap.

In class, I will ask a claims adjuster to come up to the front of the room and explain some process where they have to give a lot of information. While they're doing that, every time they give a particular fact, I hold up a finger, and hold up an additional finger for every additional fact they give me. Of course I'm having them face the other way while they give the information, so they don't see it, and I show the class exactly how this works. Here's an example.

I'll ask a claims adjuster to give me information on what's going to happen to my claim after she's already gathered all the information. It usually goes something like this. The adjuster, let's call her Kathy Smith, is facing the other side of the room and I'm standing behind her.

Kathy starts her explanation, "Well, Carl, here's what's going to happen on the claim from this point forward: I'm going to send someone out to your house (one finger), and he's going to write an estimate (two), and he's going to give you a copy (three). You can go ahead and take that estimate to any body shop you'd like (four) and if they have any questions they can call me (five), or call the person who wrote the estimate (six). If at any time you need a rental car (seven), then give me a call at this number (eight). Now, since you were injured in this accident (nine), I'm going to send out a medical authorization (ten). I'd like you to sign it and send it back to me (eleven).

Right about that time, I'll stop Kathy and ask the class how Kathy was doing. Usually everybody will say, "Oh she's doing great." Then I ask them an important question: "What was I doing behind Kathy's back?" People will say "counting". Counting what? Counting the time? No. Counting the number of "ums?" No. Usually someone will get around to saying, "counting the facts." That's right, I was counting the facts. What did I get up to? Well in this case I got up to number eleven, and we weren't done yet. We still had to explain lots more information, so we're at fact number eleven, on our way to thirty, easy.

Let me ask you, the reader, how many facts do you think people can hold in their conscious mind at any given time? Not how many things can you remember, but how many things can you hold in your conscience mind at any given time? Think of it this way, how many things can you think of at the same time? For most of us, it's two, maybe if you're particularly bright, three. I'm sure there's an idiot savant out there who can hold four. But for most of us it's two, maybe three. As a customer, how many did I just get? I just got eleven, on my way to thirty.

The problem with this is, if you give information this way: fact, fact, fact, fact, by the time you're done this person's going to remember about 20% of what you just said. Why? Because our conscious mind can only hold a couple facts at any given time. Once a fact enters our conscious mind, there are only two things that can happen to it. Either it can go down into our long term memory, or it can go out of our head, never to be remembered again. What happens is, since our conscious mind can only hold a couple facts at a time, unless you force the person to make a judgment on the information as you go, then it works very much like First In, First Out, (FIFO) inventory.

The first fact comes in, no problem. The second fact comes in, no problem. The third fact comes in, what happened to the first one? Out of their head. The fourth fact comes in, what happens to number two, out of their head. The fifth fact comes in, number three, out of their head. And you're just shifting information.

And when you finally finish, this person is going to remember about 20% of what you just said. Why? Because you're just shifting information. Unless you force them to make a judgment on the information as you go.

Awesome Adjusters know the normal way of just dishing out information, fact after fact, doesn't work very well. They have a slightly different technique. They know there is a way to give information that would automatically increase someone's retention level from 20%, to maybe 60% or 70%? Would that be helpful for you? Would that save you some time?

That would be helpful any time you must explain information to someone who doesn't quite get it and you have to re-explain it. For most of us adjusters, it probably would be a great help. And to be able to do that is relatively simple.

But before I teach you how to increase a customer's retention from 20% to maybe 60% or 70%, let me pose another question. Would it be helpful if people were listening while you were talking? If the answer is yes, then I want to go back to whether you have an effect on that. Yes, you do.

Right now, in claims, the way we give information, we're doing things that make people stop listening to us. Through the years of monitoring phone calls, I can say with certainty that people stop listening for two major reasons. Just two. And if we know what they are and can be careful to avoid them, we will make our job so much easier.

MAKING PEOPLE LISTEN

The number one reason people stop listening is because we say something they object to. We either ask them to do something or conclude something that makes sense to us, however, for whatever reason, they object to it.

I found that the second reason people stop listening is because we spew jargon that they don't understand; maybe a word or a phrase that they don't understand. Using terms like as "first party claim," or "issue you a draft," or "mitigate your damage." All of these things sound normal to us, but if the customer doesn't automatically understand them, he/she will stop listening and get hung up on some word or phrase.

Here is an example. Let's return to what Kathy was saying to her customer. Let's say Kathy is talking to me, a customer who, for whatever reason, doesn't want anyone coming to his house. Who knows why? Maybe I was robbed three years ago, who knows? Tell me, what happens inside my head when Kathy says:

> *Well, Carl, here's what's going to happen on the claim from this point forward: I'm going to send someone out to your house, and he's going to write an estimate on your car, and he's going to give you a copy. You can go ahead and take that estimate to any body shop you'd like, and if they have any questions, they can call me or call the person who wrote the estimate. If at any time you need a rental car, then give me a call at this number . . . blah . . . blah . . . blah.*

What happened in my head as soon as she told me someone is coming to my house? I stopped listening. That's right! I have not heard a single word she has said. Do you know what I was doing while she was talking? That's right. I was formulating my reply. I'm about to object, but I'll wait until she's done talking. In the meantime, I haven't heard a single word she has said after that, and Kathy is completely wasting her time.

Of course, Kathy will find this out soon enough. Because when she's done, I will raise the issue about coming to my house, and Kathy will solve it by agreeing to meet at the body shop. Then I will start asking questions about things Kathy mentioned after that, and Kathy will think to herself, "Man, why don't customers listen?"

Here is a serious question. What are the odds that Kathy is going to be able to explain something to her customer, using thirty facts in a row, in a process that the customer doesn't understand, that Kathy's not going to say a single thing that that customer doesn't object to? And that every word Kathy uses the customer will understand? What are the odds of this? Well, in the case of explaining the claims process, the odds are probably very low.

When we go through a long explanation with a customer, invariably we'll say something either they object to, or that they don't understand, and at that point they're not listening anymore. The downfall is, we don't know they stopped listening, and we just keep talking.

What if there was a technique that would automatically tell you when someone has stopped listening to you? Even while you're talking. While you're talking, you would know if they're not listening to you anymore. Would that be helpful to you? Sure! Because what would you do if you knew someone wasn't listening to you while you were talking? You'd stop talking and figure out the problem, wouldn't you?

Well, we're going to be able to achieve both those things we've talked about. We're going to be able to know when someone isn't listening, and increase their retention rate from 20% to maybe 60% or 70% using a technique that Kathy uses. You see, I know Kathy Smith. She's awesome. She's an Awesome Adjuster. And Kathy would never give out information by dishing out fact after fact. Kathy uses a little technique called nail down questions.

NAIL DOWN QUESTIONS

A nail down question is any question to which the answer is "yes." Often times salespeople will get this in their training classes. They are taught how to do this, although sometimes they do a poor job of applying it. They might say something like, "Isn't that a great television? Don't you love that picture? Isn't that a great price? Isn't that a good-looking case? Don't you love that remote?" And they ask you these questions to get you to say what? "Yes."

That's right; they are trying to get you to say "yes." Why are they doing this, are they just wasting their time? There are plenty of people who absolutely believe that if you can get a customer to say "yes," five, six, seven, maybe eight times is a row, then they are more likely to buy. Why? Well, number one, it puts the customer in the mood of agreement. So when it comes time to ask for the sale, they are more likely to say yes because they are in the mood of agreement.

Number two, however, much more important for the Awesome Adjuster, is that it forces the person to make a judgment on the information. Since you've forced that person to process that information, instead of going out of their head, they are more likely to remember it, because they've had to do something with it. Remember back a few pages, we said when you give customers many facts in a row, that unless you force them to make a judgment on the information as you go, their retention works very much like First in, First out inventory.

Here's a real-life example. I was listening in on a phone conversation and a claims adjuster was giving information to a customer, by saying something like the following: "Mr. Burke, we are going to send David Lewin out from Haig & Lewin to write an estimate on the damage to your house. He'll give you a copy of that estimate, and you can take that to any contractor you'd like. If they have any questions, you can call me or Dave. If you need to stay in a hotel while the work is being done, please give me a call and I will set up a direct bill with our local hotel. We have an agreement with them to keep the bills coming directly to us and that helps keep the costs down. Since you lost some personal property, I'd like to send you an inventory sheet. You'll need to fill out that form, sign it, and send it back to me. Once I get that form, I will look for the replacement cost of those items. I will review them for accuracy, and if they are covered under your policy I will pay them. If they are not covered under the policy, I'll either send you a letter or contact you by phone. Now, about your deductible . . . "

Let's go ahead and go through that and count the facts. How many did you count? Well actually, there were twenty-three facts in that statement. Keep in mind that the sentence "Mr. Burke, we are going to send David Lewin (1) out from Haig & Lewin (2) to write an estimate on the damage to your house (3)" has three facts all by itself.

Unfortunately, the way that information was given there is absolutely no way that person will remember any more than the last few things that that claims adjuster said. Why? Since the conscious mind can only hold two or three facts at any given time, it works very much like First Out inventory. The first fact comes in, no problem. The second fact comes in, no problem. The third fact comes in, and what happens to the first one? Out. The fourth fact comes in, the second fact goes out. The fifth fact comes in, the third fact goes out. And by the time this adjuster is done, he's just shifted information, and this person is only going to remember about 20% of what he just said.

Here's how Kathy might change that conversation:

Kathy: *Dr. Burke, we are going to send David Lewin out from Haig &*
           Lewin to write an estimate on the damage to your house. Does that
           sound all right?

Dr. Burke: *Yes.*

Kathy: *He'll give you a copy of that estimate and you can take that to any*
           contractor you'd like. If they have any questions, you can call me
           or Dave. Sound good?

Dr. Burke: *Uh-huh.*

Kathy: *If you need to stay in a hotel while the work is being done, please*
           give me a call and I will set up or a direct bill with our local hotel.
           We have an agreement with them to keep the bills coming directly
           to us and that helps keep the costs down. Make sense?

Dr. Burke: *Yep.*

Kathy: *Since you lost some personal property, I'd like to send you an*
           inventory sheet. You'll need to fill out that form, sign it, and send

it back to me. Would that be okay?

Dr. Burke: *Okay.*

Kathy: *Once I get that form, I will look for the replacement cost of those items. I will review them for accuracy, and if they are covered under your policy, I will pay them. If they are not covered under the policy, I'll either send you a letter or contact you by phone. Sound Okay?*

Dr. Burke: *Yes.*

Kathy: *Do you have any questions?*

Notice in this case how Kathy broke up the stream of information every two, maybe three facts with a nail down question? It didn't have to be a long, drawn-out question or anything like that. Just a simple question to get a response. When a customer responds to your prompting, that person obviously must be processing that information as opposed to letting it go out of their head. That will force the information down to the long-term memory much better than if they don't have to process that information. By the time you are done, you will have increased this person's retention from 20% to maybe 60% - 70%.

Now let's say in another conversation an adjuster said, "I'm going to send out a medical form for you to complete and send back, is that alright?" The customer responded with "No." Would that be a problem for us? Would that be a bad thing? It wouldn't necessarily be a bad thing because now we know we said something either the person objected to or they didn't understand. And now, instead of talking when they are not listening, we can go back and solve it.

So now what question do we ask when they say "No?" We might ask, "What is it that you don't understand?" Or, "What is it that doesn't sound okay?"; or, "What is it that doesn't make sense?"

What I hear most often when a customer does not hear or understand what the adjuster is saying, is the adjuster simply repeating what they've just said. Here's an example. I was listening to a conversation between a claims adjuster and an insured.

Karissa: *Laura, do you have the same coverage on this car as you did on the Lexus?*

Laura: *Coverages?*

Karissa: *Yes, coverages. Are they the same on this car as they were on the Lexus?*

Laura: *Are the coverages the same?*

Karissa: *(Sounding annoyed) Yes. The coverages on your car, ARE THEY THE SAME?*

Laura: *Uh . . . Yeah . . . do I get a rental?*

In listening to this conversation do you believe Laura, the customer, understood what Karissa was really trying to say? No, the customer just finally felt stupid so she pretended that she did. She didn't understand at all. I hear conversations like this quite a bit where adjusters are explaining something to customers and when the customer doesn't understand, the adjuster simply repeats himself. Then the customer is forced to try to figure out what the adjuster was talking about and usually they guess wrong.

This is where the use of nail down questions comes in. And it is very important. If an Awesome Adjuster asks a customer, "Does that make sense?" or, "Does that sound alright?" or, "Do you understand?" and the person responding says "No," instead of repeating himself, the Awesome Adjuster responds with, "What is it that you don't understand?"

The reason for that is obvious; just repeating yourself won't help them understand, because it didn't help the first time. Saying whatever you said didn't work the first time, so repeating it has no value. An Awesome Adjuster does a good job of finding out what it is, so they can solve the problem.

What you don't want to do with nail down questions is to repeat yourself over and over again using the same question. Anything can be tedious if you say it over and over again. If you say to a person "Do you understand?" "Do you understand?" "Do you understand?" ten times is a row, what are they going to say to you? They are going to say, "Of course I understand, what do you think I am, a moron?"

The effective way to use nail down questions is to break up the conversation with very simple prompts to get an answer, without repeating yourself over and over again. Something like, "Makes sense?" "Sound alright?" "Are you with me so far?" "Sound good?" Anything along those lines. You are simply trying to get them to respond.

Even if they grunt. Even if after you say, "Does that sound alright" they say, "Uugh." That's fine. You've got what you wanted, you got a response. If they say no, then all you have to do is figure out what the problem is and solve it.

Why do we ask "yes" questions instead of "no" questions? It's very simple. Many people believe that human beings simply remember things better when they have agreed with the information rather than disagreed. It's no big deal, but it might be better to ask questions that solicit "yes" if they understand, rather than "no" if they don't.

What you don't want to do if you are explaining something that has a lot of facts and detail, is to ask negative questions such as, "Do you have a problem with that?" or, "Do you have any concerns with that?" The reason you don't ask those questions is because it plants a seed in their mind and makes them think of any reason why they should disagree with the information. That is not what you are after.

Right now you are just trying to get them to remember what you are saying, not come up with reasons to argue. So instead of saying, "Do you have a problem with that?" try, "Is that alright?" And of course you should save the golden question of, "Do you have any questions?" until the end.

Now keep in mind that nail down questions do not convince anyone that you are right; they only help them remember what you say, and help you know when they stop listening. It does not convince them that you are right. That is something we will learn later.

DON'T TRY THIS AT HOME

I was contacted one time after a training class that I did in Santa Barbara by a person who was very enthusiastic about what I had taught that day. They contacted me about three weeks after the class and they said, "Carl, you know those nail down questions, they really work. I think it's a great tool. But they don't work 100% of the time." And I said, "What do you mean?" And he said, "Well, I was talking to my wife . . . "(right then I knew that was trouble, but I wanted to hear the story anyway).

He continued with, "Usually my wife and I go out to dinner on Friday, and then afterward go to the movies. I like to go bowling but my wife likes to go to the movies instead. So this time I thought I'd use the nail down questions to see if I could get my way. So I called her up and I said, 'Honey, you know that we always go to dinner on Friday and then out to the movies. But this Friday after dinner, I'd like to go bowling. Are you with me so far?'"

Needless to say, his conversation with his wife didn't go too well after that, I'm sure. The point is, that person tried to use nail down questions to try to convince someone that they are right, which it doesn't do at all. It simply gets them to remember what you said. There's no doubt in my mind that that gentleman's wife will never forget what he said. And he's going to spend a lot of time wishing she would.

One of the most effective time management techniques for Awesome

Adjusters is the way that they gain cooperation from people. They do an excellent job of gaining cooperation from their co-workers, their customers, even their managers. They have a very effective tool for being persuasive, which I will go into in our next chapter of Interpersonal Skills.

CHAPTER 5

Interpersonal Skills

Before we can discuss the right way to be persuasive, we must rule out the wrong way to be persuasive, and that is what I lovingly refer to as "the claims hammer."

THE CLAIMS HAMMER

As adjusters we constantly need to gain cooperation from people. Many people in other disciplines in their daily lives don't need to work too hard in order to gain cooperation from people. Grocery store clerks, for example, don't need to convince customers that they need to go pick out their items and bring them to him/her. They don't need to convince the customer that they need to take the items out of the basket and put them on the belt to be scanned. They don't need to convince anyone that when they ring up the total they should pay for it.

A grocery store clerk may, however, have to convince a customer that the coupons that they are using aren't the right ones. Or that just because an item is mispriced, doesn't mean the customer is entitled to get the item for that price, or a number of other things.

Many other industries, however, involve a bit of convincing. A retail clerk might need to convince a customer that they have to fill out a form in order to have a product shipped to them. A doctor's receptionist might have to convince a patient to complete a medical evaluation form in order to be seen by the doctor. There is an endless list of examples when people in other industries have to convince someone to cooperate with them. However, they do not come close to how often we in claims are asked to perform this delicate task.

In fact, of all the time an adjuster will spend negotiating, I'll bet only 10% of that time is spent negotiating for the dollar value of something. The other 90% is spent negotiating for something else. Cooperation.

Adjusters spend an incredible amount of time just negotiating for cooperation. Either trying to convince a customer to mail in an estimate so that they can get paid, or sign a medical authorization so we can get the bills, or even to give a recorded statement. Unfortunately, most of us in claims go about the process exactly the opposite way that it is most effective. We pull out the claims hammer.

The claims hammer is the tool we pull out to convince someone to cooperate with us. The object is to inflict so much pain that there is no way the person can stand it so they finally do what we ask them to do.

Let's take the example where a claims adjuster, Suzanne, is trying to get someone, Mr. Wimsatt, to send them an estimate. The conversation might go like this:

Suzanne: *Mr. Wimsatt, in order for me to handle your claim, I need you to go out and get an estimate of the damage to your car.*

Mr. Wimsatt: *I'm not doing that, no way.*

Suzanne: *Well if you don't, there's no way I can pay you.* (Whack!)

Once again, the approach in order to gain cooperation is to pull out the claims hammer and start whacking away. You might ask yourself, "Why is this the wrong tool? This works." People do cooperate when we inflict pain on them. My response is, of course it works. The problem with the claims hammer is not that it doesn't work; the problem with it is that it works just fine.

We can inflict pain on people so they cooperate with us. However, once you gain cooperation by inflicting pain on a customer, all you have now is an angry customer who's going to try to get back at you at every turn. It's going to be why they don't cooperate with you, it's going to be why they question everything you do, it's why they're going to challenge everything that you say. Because you pushed them into doing something they didn't want to do, because you could, because you are stronger than they are.

What is this claims hammer we love to pull out? Well, usually it is the facts. We love to hit people with the facts. We do it all the time in claims. Do any of these sound familiar: "I know you want $20 per day, but your policy says $15" (Whack); "The law says we only owe you a comparable vehicle" (Whack); "You are not entitled to a new one, you only paid for an ACV policy" (Whack).

We used force, and because we are stronger than they are, and we have a big claims hammer, and we whacked them until they couldn't take the pain anymore, they finally did what we asked them to do. But, we now have a built-in enemy.

Usually, the claims hammer will work. However, most often it is not the right tool. I propose that there is another tool that can be used. The tool Awesome Adjusters pull out, before the claims hammer, is the "Why" tool. That's right, a simple question, one word, "Why."

Let me demonstrate the value of this tool. I was listening in on a conversation in a claims office, and the adjuster was trying to settle a total loss with a customer. The adjuster had his array of facts, including a fair market evaluation report completed by a company called CCC. It showed the value of the customer's vehicle to be about $2,500. The adjuster calls up the customer, and here is what I heard:

Adjuster: *Mr. Blasz, I have the fair market evaluation back on your car and it turns out that your car is worth $2,500. We'd like to pay you $2,500 to settle your claim.*

Mr. Blasz: *No, I really feel my car is worth $3,000.*

Adjuster: *Well, I have a CCC report that says it's worth $2,500. (Whack!)*

Mr. Blasz: *Well, I still feel my car is worth $3,000.*

Adjuster: *Mr. Blasz, you know if you don't take the $2,500, we can't pay the storage charges on your car anymore. (Whack!)*

Mr. Blasz: *Look, I understand, but I still feel my car is worth $3,000.*

Adjuster: *If we don't settle this today, we're not going to be able to pay for your rental car any longer either. (Whack!)*

Mr. Blasz: *Look, like I said, I really feel my car is worth $3,000.*

Adjuster: *Okay, but if you don't take the offer, you're still going to have to pay your car payment. (Whack!)*

Of course listening to this, I knew that the adjuster was going to have a difficult time settling this case, which he didn't do in that conversation. So I went out to the adjuster after this conversation, and I said, "You know, I think if you would have changed your process just barely, I think you could have settled this case. See, you're trying to convince this person to give in. It's much easier to convince someone you're right, than it is to get them to give in if they think you are wrong."

The adjuster looked at me, shrugged his shoulders and said, "He'll get tired of walking."

You know what? That adjuster is right, that customer will get tired of walking. In a week, he's going to call up and say, "Fine I'll take your stupid $2,500." In the meantime, he will have trashed the company's name all over the place, called up three times to make complaints, and caused a tremendous amount of time and trouble for this adjuster. The claims hammer will work, it'll work just fine. But, it will take a lot of time to inflict so much pain on the person before they finally give in, that it's a big time-waster and very big loss of customer service.

Guess what question this adjuster never asked the customer, not one single time? That's right, he never asked him "Why." He never said, "Why do you feel your car is worth $3,000?" He never even asked.

The adjuster never asked Why because he has his claims hammer and it works just fine. What does he care what the customer's reasons are? He's going to win this fight. He's got his claims hammer, and he will whack away at this customer until he surrenders. And when he does, the adjuster will think to himself, "Man, am I ever a good negotiator!"

As you read this, let me ask you, are you curious why this customer wanted $3,000? Well I certainly was. I was dying of curiosity. So you know what I did? I did something I almost never do, I called this customer and I talked to him.

I called up the customer (not really Mr. Blasz, that's just an attorney friend of mine) and I said, "Hello, my name is Carl Van and I was monitoring the phone call you were just on for quality assurance, I hope you don't mind." Of course Mr. Blasz bitched at me for the next 15 minutes and said things like, "Yeah? Well, you guys suck."

But after a few minutes he calmed down a little bit, and I was able to get some information out of him. By the end of the conversation I said, "Okay, thanks Mr. Blasz, I appreciate the information. Oh, and by the way, I'm just curious, why do you feel your car is worth $3,000?"

You know, the answer to that question had nothing to do with any CCC fair market evaluation report. It had nothing to do with car payments. It had nothing to do with storage charges. And it certainly had nothing to do with his staying in a rental car. The reason this customer wanted $3,000 for his car had absolutely nothing to do with what the adjuster was literally beating him to death with. The adjuster just didn't know it because he didn't pull out the right tool; he never asked why.

Guess what he did pull out? He pulled out his claims hammer and started whacking away. And in a week he's going to settle this case and feel like he did his job. The downfall is, he's taken much, much more time than he ever had to if he had pulled out the right tool. He could have pulled out "why," but he didn't.

You know what this customer said to me when I asked him why he wanted $3,000? He said, "Look, my brother gave me that car, and he died about six months ago. It's all I have from him. And I know someone had recently offered him $3,000 for it, and I'm not going to let you guys rip him off."

Can you imagine the feelings this customer has wrapped up in this car? Do you think there is any way this customer is going to be swayed by storage charges? Think about it. If this customer was to accept anything less than $3,000, then he would be letting an insurance company rip off his dead brother. Is this customer going to be convinced by rental charges? Is he going to give in because the adjuster brought up car payments? Of course not. The adjuster will never know it, because he simply never asked why. He had his claims hammer, and he used it.

There's an old saying and it goes like this: when all you have is a hammer, everything looks like a nail. Guess what that means? It's very simple. It doesn't matter if you need a saw, it doesn't matter if you need a pair of pliers, and it certainly doesn't matter if you need sand paper. If all you have is a hammer, you're going to use it, even if it's the wrong tool. Why? Because it's all you've got. And what do you do with hammers? You hit things with them.

We in claims often times try to convince other people to do what we want by pulling out the claims hammer and inflicting pain on them. We don't mean it literally to cause them pain, but in effect that's what it does. By telling someone what will happen to them, if they don't do what we ask them, we are inflicting pain upon that person.

I would like to submit this. To tell someone, "Here's how this will hurt you if you don't do this" will get a different reaction than, "Here's how this will help you if you do this." These are two completely different things. They both gain cooperation, but one doesn't start a war like the other one does.

Funny thing with the tool "Why," is that even if we ask the other person why, we often still resort to our pounding away with the claims hammer. Let's return to that original conversation where the adjuster wanted the customer to get an estimate. Here is how the call went:

Suzanne: *Mr. Wimsatt, I need you to go out and get an estimate on your car and send it in.*

Mr. Wimsatt: *No way, I'm not doing that.*

Suzanne: *Well if you don't, there's no way I can pay you.* (Whack!)

Mr. Wimsatt: *Look, I'm not going to go get that estimate.*

Suzanne: *Why not?*

Mr. Wimsatt: *Look, I'm the victim here. I'm the one whose car got hit. Why should I run around doing your job?*

Suzanne: *Mr. Wimsatt, it's not my job to get an estimate. If you want your car fixed and you want to get paid, you're going to have to go get an estimate* (Whack!)

Mr. Wimsatt: *I'm not doing it.*

Suzanne: *Why not?*

Mr. Wimsatt: *Look, you guys ran into me, I'm the victim here, not you. I'm not running around and getting estimates for this.*

Suzanne: *Well if you don't, I can't pay you.* (Whack!)

Notice a couple of things. The first thing I want you to notice is the adjuster finally did pull out her "Why" tool, but after annoying the customer. First she gave him a nice big whack with her claims hammer, before even bothering to ask why. Most of the time, we will ask the person Why, eventually. Unfortunately, it's not our first response, our first response is to give them a nice big whack with our claims hammers, and then if it occurs to us, we will finally ask Why. But by that time the process of the argument has already started.

Notice the second thing. After the adjuster asked Why, she went right back to using her claims hammer.

I'm going to make a statement now that you the reader will probably disagree with. I haven't provided you with enough evidence to convince you, but perhaps by the end of this book I will. However I want to bring up the point now, just to lay the groundwork.

I've had the opportunity to monitor phone calls and make observations all over the country, in many different claims offices. If you do nothing but listen to phone calls in claims offices, you are bound to hear arguments. Based on my observations: most arguments are started by the claims person, who didn't hear what the customer just said. And I mean what they just said. Most arguments could be completely avoided if both parties actually heard what the other person was saying.

Take the example above. When the adjuster finally does ask why, the person told her why, which is what the adjuster reacted to. The adjuster reacted to what she thought he heard, which is "Why should I do your job?" Unfortunately, what she didn't hear was that this person just called himself a victim. This guy used the word victim to describe himself.

This person said, "I'm not going to do that, I'm the victim here, why should I run around doing your job?" The key words were not the question about the job, which is what the adjuster heard, but the fact that this person called himself a victim.

While I was listening to this conversation, it was rather clear to me right away, this person was clearly saying why he wouldn't cooperate. He used the word victim to describe himself. What do we normally associate the word victim with? Usually it's associated with a crime of some sort. This person is using the same word that he might use to describe himself in the event he was held up or robbed or attacked in some way. He is using the word "victim" to describe himself.

And the funny thing about it is, he's perfectly justified in feeling that way. The way he sees it, he wasn't doing anything wrong. Someone ran into him while he was minding his own business, and now he's the one who is going to have to miss a day of work; now he's the one who's going to have to run around and get his damage estimated; and he's the one who's being inconvenienced. None of this is fair, and for him to feel like a victim is perfectly reasonable. The problem is the adjuster didn't hear that, she heard, "Why should I have to run around doing your job?"

What should have been that adjuster's response? Well I could tell you that even if she had heard the person using the word victim, she likely still would have pulled out her claims hammer as we all would and now try to convince the person that they are wrong. We are going to try to convince them that they are wrong for the way they feel. And we are going to say something along the lines of, "Oh no, you're not a victim, you shouldn't feel that way."

Can you ever change the way someone feels by giving them a bunch of facts? It usually doesn't work, and it usually makes them feel stupid and then they dig in and then you have two issues. You are trying to change the way they feel, and they don't want to feel stupid.

Most of us do a very good job of listing a bunch of facts, figures, and reason why someone should change the way they feel. Unfortunately, that doesn't work very well. So why do we use it? Because it's the only tool we have. We don't have any other tool, so we pull out the claims hammer and we start whacking away with facts and figures, trying to change the way someone feels. I gave you the first tool, which is the question why. Now I would like to give you the second tool that might actually work in changing the way someone feels.

If you are a fan of the show "Seinfeld" like I am, you will remember an episode where George concludes that every single decision and every single approach he made in his past, was wrong. Every gut instinct he had had always led him to disaster. So he incorporates a new philosophy: if every single thing that he had ever done was wrong, then the opposite must be right. And from that point forward, instead of doing what he would normally do, he does the exact opposite. Of course things work out very well for him. He gets a new girlfriend, he gets a new job, and his life becomes quite blissful (for a while).

I'm not suggesting that philosophy, but I am suggesting that in order to be persuasive, we pull out the claims hammer, which is the exact opposite of what we usually use. Most of us tend to pull out the claims hammer and start whacking away when we are trying to convince someone of our point of view. In fact, we will be very detailed in pulling out their beliefs and hitting them with our claims hammer so hard that they give in. Keep in mind once again, I'm not saying this doesn't work, I'm just saying that you will have a battle on your hands that you don't need to have.

The opposite of hitting a customer with a claims hammer to get them to give in from the pain is to simply acknowledge where they are coming from. Awesome Adjusters use the tool of acknowledgement to gain cooperation and save time.

ACKNOWLEDGEMENT: THE REAL POWER TOOL

Yes, the claims hammer is a pretty good tool, and as a matter of fact in some cases it might be the right one, but what I am about to talk about now is what

I refer to as a power tool. A power tool does the same job as the original tool, but much more effectively and efficiently. The power tool that can change the way someone feels is Acknowledgement.

In the event you are trying to be persuasive, the first two steps are pretty clear. The first is to ask the question why, and the second one is to acknowledge the person's point of view.

I would like to propose a maxim in claims. A maxim is a truth to be held. The maxim I would like to propose is this: people will accept what you have to say, to the exact degree you demonstrate you know where they are coming from.

Through the years of observing interactions, I've found this to be very true. People will accept what you have to say to the exact degree you demonstrate you know where they are coming from. Let's take a look at this.

In the previous example, the adjuster clearly started an argument by pulling out the claims hammer and whacking away at this customer who didn't want to go get an estimate. Watch how the tempo of the conversation changes if the adjuster uses the right tool. Teresa George knew how to use this tool (no, not Mother Teresa . . . this is a different Teresa). Today she is a Claims Manager for a national insurance carrier. But at one time she was one of my adjusters. Here is how she would have handled it:

Teresa: *Mr. Wimsatt, I need you to go out and get an estimate on your car and send it in.*

Mr. Wimsatt: *No way, I'm not doing that.*

Teresa: *Uh, okay, can you tell me why?*

Mr. Wimsatt: *Because you guys ran into me, I'm the victim here, why should I run around doing your job?*

Teresa: *Mr. Wimsatt, if you don't want to go get an estimate, because you are feeling like a victim right now, I can understand that. I know you weren't doing anything wrong, and feel dragged into this thing that you didn't want to be in. Now you are being asked to take the time to try to deal with all this. If you feel that that's unfair, and if you feel like the victim, I completely understand that; that's very reasonable.*

Notice what Teresa did in this case. She completely reduced the person's anger by acknowledging it. Notice she did not agree with it, and notice she did not say "Yes, you are right, you are a victim." She simply acknowledged where the person was coming from. She called the customer a reasonable person. He's reasonable for the way he feels. The fact that Teresa took the time to tell this customer that he was a reasonable person for the way he feels is going to turn this person's feelings around.

Now, the more closely Teresa ties what she wants the customer to do with the customer changing the way he feels, the more likely he will do it. Let me repeat, the more closely Teresa ties what she wants the customer to do, to the customer changing his feelings, the more likely the customer is to do it. Watch how Teresa uses this tool.

Teresa: *Mr. Wimsatt, if you don't want to go get an estimate, because you are feeling like a victim right now, I can understand that. I know you weren't doing anything wrong, and feel dragged into this thing that you didn't want to be in. Now you are being asked to take the time to try to deal with all this. If you feel that that's unfair, and if you feel like the victim, I completely understand that; that's very reasonable.*

I'll tell you what though. If you are able to go out and get an estimate, some good things will happen. Number one, you'll be able to pick the body shop of your choice. Number two, you'll be able to be there when they write the estimate so that you can point out any damage that someone else might miss. And number three, if

83

you can send me this estimate right away as opposed to my having to wait for someone else to mail it in, I will do everything I can to get this payment issued to you. Finally, and most importantly, once this is paid, and your car is repaired, and all of this is over and done with, perhaps you won't have to feel like a victim anymore. Would you be willing to go get this estimate so that I can help you?

Notice how Teresa in this case, ties in this person changing the way they feel to what she wants him to do. Once the customer does what Teresa wants him to do, he won't have to feel like a victim anymore. Teresa actually heard what the person said about his feeling like a victim and used it to her advantage.

The idea of acknowledgement is extremely important. Rather than trying to convince someone they're wrong, it's much easier to convince them you understand where they are coming from. Remember our maxim: people will accept what you have to say to the exact degree you demonstrate you know where they are coming from.

Here's a real life example. I was in Cincinnati, Ohio, one time to teach a class, when I got a call from a friend. He called me up and asked if I could help him find a hotel room because he couldn't find one anywhere in Cincinnati, and he had to come out there that night to teach a class the next day. He was running off to go teach another class and didn't have time right then, so he asked for my help. I told him I would try to help him out.

After we hung up, I dialed the 800 number right on the phone of the hotel I was staying at. I told the operator at the 800 number that I needed a room tonight in the hotel where I was because a friend of mine was coming into town. That person responded by saying, "Oh, no problem, we've got plenty of rooms, we're not even one-third booked. Just bring the person in tonight and they'll be sure to get a room. You don't need to make a reservation."

With that, I contacted my friend and left him a message saying, "Don't worry; we've got plenty of room at my hotel." At the time I kind of wondered why I was able to get a room so easily when he had so much trouble, but I went off to teach my class, and I forgot about it.

After my class, I went to the airport and I picked him up and we went back to the hotel. We both walked right up to the counter and I said to the counter person there, "Yes, hello, this is a friend of mine who needs a room for tonight and I called earlier and they said you had plenty of rooms." The hotel clerk looked at his screen for a minute or two, shook his head and said, "You know, we're completely booked."

Obviously I was annoyed and I responded, "No, no, no, I called the 800 number this morning and they said you had plenty of rooms." His response was, "Sir, we have no rooms, we're completely booked."

Getting angry, I said, "Look, you don't understand, this puts me in very bad situation. I've got my friend here who I told I would get a room. Now because I told him I could get him a room, he probably didn't go look for himself when he could have found a room in the meantime. Now we are both standing here and he doesn't have a room, and I feel responsible. I feel like a complete jerk."

The desk clerk takes the terminal, turns it around and points to the screen, and says, "Sir, we have no more rooms!" He said this to me like he was calling me an idiot. "Look at the absolute truth, look at the undisputed evidence that there are no rooms, you idiot," is what I felt like he was trying to tell me.

All this did was infuriate me, so I said, "Look, let me talk to a manager, I want to talk to a manager right now!" And he said, "Okay," walked a few steps away, and said, "Hey, Amanda, this guy wants to talk to you."

Now I know the words 'this guy' is code for something. It probably starts with an A, but, hey, that's just a random guess. So when he said, 'this guy wants to talk to you,' I already knew I was being set up for an argument.

The next thing I know, Amanda, a psychology student, walks over to us both and says, "Yes, may I help you?" And I said, "Yes, this is my friend. I called the 800 number this morning and asked to make a reservation. They told me they had plenty of rooms, and there would be no problem. Now I've picked him up at the airport and we are standing here and we are being told you have no rooms. I feel like an idiot and my friend is out of a room. That's just not right! So what's up?"

Amanda pauses for a moment while she looks at the screen, and replies, "Oh, Mr. Van. I'm so sorry. I'm sorry for the difficult situation you've been put in. We don't have any rooms; the person you were talking to at the 800 number must have been looking at the wrong screen, because we have been booked for over a week. I'm so sorry for your inconvenience. I understand the difficulty you are going through, and I understand the position you are in. Believe me, if we had a room right now, I would give it to you. I really would. The truth is, I just don't have a room to actually give to you. I would if I could, I just can't. Can I help you find a room somewhere else?"

Now let me ask, of these two people who both told me "no," who was more believable? The person who threw the facts in my face with the screen being the reason I should believe him? Or Amanda, who said she was sorry and understood where I was coming from?

Probably Amanda. Amanda seemed much more credible because she understood where I was coming from. She said she understood the difficult situation I was in, and if she had a room, she'd give it to me. That seemed believable to me. I believed, they actually were full because she understood where I was coming from, and she was able to relate that to me.

If she had just said something along the lines of, "Yeah, I'm really sorry, there's nothing I can do," that would not have seemed as believable. The statement "I want to help you, and I would if I could, I just can't," is much more powerful than "I won't help you because I don't have to."

The idea here is to use acknowledgement as a way to get someone to believe what you are about to say. What are you acknowledging? You're acknowledging that the other person is a reasonable person for their beliefs or for their circumstance. You are not saying you agree with them, you are not saying they are right, you're simply saying that you understand where they are coming from. They are reasonable for their beliefs.

Let's apply these to another situation. Sarah Holton is great at this. Sarah is Director of Claims and Assistant Vice President at one of the largest international insurance companies. But once upon a time she was a claims adjuster working for me. Here is how she would handle a situation like this.

Sarah: *Mr. Dudenhofer, in order to get your medical bills, you're going to need to fill out this form.*

Mr. Dudenhofer: *I don't want to do that.*

Sarah: *Would you mind telling me why?*

Mr. Dudenhofer: *Yeah, because I was told I wouldn't have to sign anything.*

Sarah: *Mr. Dudenhofer, if you don't want to fill out this Medical Authorization because you were told you wouldn't have to sign anything, I understand that, that's reasonable. Whoever told you that was mistaken, and I am very sorry about that. I don't know why you were told that. Maybe they were just trying to reassure you nothing would happen without your permission, I really don't know. The truth is, I'd like you to fill out this form so I can get your medical bills paid. If you can fill out this form and return it to me, I will do everything I can to make sure I get everything I need to process your claim. But again, I do understand that you were given the wrong information and I am sorry. Would you be willing to fill out these forms so I can help you?*

Did that sound better? Is it possible that this customer might be a little bit more cooperative right now? This customer is not going to be Mr. Sunshine.

He's not going to sit there and say, "Oh boy, am I glad I got the wrong information now, thank you!" But you know what? He's a little more satisfied; he's a little calmer. He has been treated with respect and most importantly, his feelings have been acknowledged as reasonable.

He is much more open to change than he would have been if Sarah had argued with him. And at the very least, even if he stays irritated, at least he won't be irritated at Sarah. And he'll probably cooperate with her and just be irritated at somebody else.

Knowing Sarah, she might have even added, "If you know who you spoke to, I can let them know that whatever they did tell you, it might have been confusing, so we don't confuse anybody else in the future. But this form is necessary and I would like to ask you to fill it out so we can help you. Would you be willing to do that so we can help?"

Can it sometimes impress a customer that you will go out of your way to solve a problem? Even if they got caught in it this time, the fact that you're willing to go out of your way to solve it for the next time, can be very impressive. But the overall tool of acknowledging where someone is coming from is a very high-powered tool and one that claims people have at their disposal at all times.

Another problem I see is adjusters not recognizing when the time to fight is over. When the battle has already been won. The ability to recognize when the time to fight is over is just as important as winning the fight. Let's take a look at that.

RECOGNIZING A GIFT WHEN YOU GET IT

Let's step away from a claims situation. Imagine a conversation between a department store clerk, Lhani, and a customer, Jennifer.

Jennifer: *Yes, I'd like to return this for a refund, please.*

88

Lhani: *Well, I can return it for you, but since it was on sale for the past week, I can only refund the sale price.*

Jennifer: *That's not fair, I paid more for this just a month ago, and it's not doing what I want it to do.*

Lhani: *I understand that. It's just that I can only refund the lowest price that we had for it in the last six months, that's our store policy. Unless you have the actual receipt for the purchase, that's our policy.*

Jennifer: *No, I don't have the receipt, but I bought it a couple of months ago for more than its sale price.*

Lhani: *I'm sorry. Our store policy is that we can only refund the amount of money that the item has been sold for. And since we don't know what that is, I have to refund just the lowest price.*

Jennifer: *That's a gyp!*

Lhani: *It's only fair because some people might come in and buy it at a lower price and then want a full refund.*

Jennifer: *I would never do anything like that!*

Lhani: *I'm not saying you would, but some people would. So that's why we do it.*

Jennifer: *I still think that's a gyp!*

Lhani: *Not really. This is what we have to do, because there's just no way of knowing what you actually paid for it. We could easily get ripped off by some people, and we are just trying to protect ourselves. That makes sense doesn't it?*

Jennifer: *It doesn't make sense to me, because now I'm going to be out $45!*

Lhani: *Well, you did use it for a month, didn't you?*

Jennifer: (getting upset) *Yes, but it didn't work right, so what good does it do me?*

Lhani: *At least you got some use out of it. That should make you feel better about losing the $45.*

Jennifer: (getting angrier) *It doesn't make me feel better at all. All I feel is that not only have I lost $45, I've wasted my time using a product that doesn't work!*

You can see that this conversation is only going to get worse. The reason it's going to get worse is because the clerk didn't realize he already had the battle won a long time ago. Remember back when the customer said, "What a gyp!" Most people would have interpreted that as a snide comment, but the Awesome Adjuster recognizes that as the gift it is. Do you know what that person is saying, when they say, "What a gyp!" Think about it just for one second, what are they really saying?

Believe it or not, what this person just said is . . . "I believe you." That's right. What this person just said is that they believe you. They're not happy about it, which is why they make the comment that it is a gyp, but nevertheless they do believe what you are telling them. There's no way for them to conclude that it's a gyp, unless they believe you first. If they didn't believe you, they'd keep arguing with you about whether or not it's really going to happen.

At this point, the Awesome Adjuster recognizes that they have convinced the person and stops all fighting. Fighting is not necessary. You don't need to inflict more pain on this person. You don't need to start an argument; this person already believes you. All you have to do from this point is empathize. You have to recognize gifts when you get them. And believe it or not, this snide comment is a gift. Take it for what it is.

Imagine the conversation going slightly differently. Let's put in Amanda. You see, although Amanda is working as a clerk in a store, she's also working toward her Ph.D. in Psychology. Here's how she handles it.

Jennifer: *Yes, I'd like to return this for a refund please.*

Amanda: *Well, I can return it for you, but since it was on sale last week, I can only refund it for the sale price.*

Jennifer: *That's not fair, I paid more for this just a month ago, and it's not doing what I want it to do.*

Amanda: *I understand that. It's just that I can only refund the lowest price that we had for it in the last six months, that's our store policy. Unless you have the actual receipt for the purchase, that's our policy.*

Jennifer: *No, I don't have the receipt but, I bought it a couple of months ago for more than its sale price.*

Amanda: *I'm sorry. Our store policy is that we can only refund the amount of money that the item has been sold for. And since we don't know what that is, I have to refund just the lowest price.*

Jennifer: *That's a gyp!* (Customer believes . . . all arguing can stop)

Amanda: (New approach) *Madam, I can understand how you feel. If it seems like a gyp I can understand that, because you are out $45. I am sorry about that. I can refund this to you in cash, or we can apply the credit to your card.*

Jennifer: *No, I'd rather have it in cash.*

Amanda: *Okay, here you go, here's your refund. Again I am sorry about the problem. And thank you for shopping with us.*

91

Jennifer: *Fine, whatever.*

What's important to understand is that this customer is not going to be thrilled. They're not happy that they lost $45, but at the very least, we don't have a clerk picking a fight with a customer. Believe it or not, because this person got treated with respect, they just may be back even though they didn't get what they wanted, and that's one of the important things to understand about customer service.

CHAPTER 6

Continuing Education

One of the hallmarks of outstanding adjusters is that they always want to improve. They see their improvement through getting better at their jobs, but they also know that it's necessary for them to seek information and study it for their own development.

Before I continue with a discussion about ways to seek out information, I'd like to describe the three types of people when it comes to continuing education.

When I am asked to come into a company and do training throughout the company at all different levels of employees, it usually involves the permission and interest of top management. When I meet with top management to discuss the aspects of the training, I am invariably asked a question such as, "How do we know that everybody will get something out of this? How do we know who to send, because we don't want to waste our time or money sending people that won't get anything out of the class? Who are the right people to send?"

My response to this is usually to explain what I call the three levels of Claims performers. When I'm asked these questions, this is my response:

THE THREE STEPS OF THE IMPROVING PERSON
(See Figure 6.1)

I say to the management executives . . .

94

Generally I find that claims people fall under three categories when it has to do with any type of training or self-improvement. When claims people are sent to a training class, or they are asked to read a book, or listen to tapes, you can generally plug them into three categories. Keep in mind these are not three equal percentages at all; it's just the main three categories. But I will try to provide some percentages so there will be some meaning.

THE RESISTERS

In the bottom level, we have the people that resist improvement. I call them the resisters. These are the people that will spend their time in a training class or after they've read a book, going around trying to convince everybody else that nothing will work. They will return from a good training class saying it wasn't valuable, they didn't get anything out of it, and it didn't mean anything at all.

For what ever reason they happen to have, they don't want to change. Maybe they don't like their manager or they feel they're underpaid, or they don't like their job, or they just feel they're terrific and they don't need improvement. They will spend time, sometimes even at a break at a training class, trying to convince other people that none of this would work, it's not valuable, and that everyone should do nothing to change.

These are usually the borderline performers. They usually are people that aren't going to achieve much anyway; they're pretty well stagnant in their position. They are doing the best they can just to hold on. They're not bad people, but they honestly do believe that the only way that they can be successful is to bring everybody else down around them. These people will spend so much of their time trying to prove to other people that nothing will work, that they will get absolutely nothing out of the class. These people are usually your low performers. Whether you want to get rid of them or not, it's up to you. But basically they will get nothing out of the class, and it will be a big waste of time. You will have wasted your money on these people.

95

THE COASTERS

Next, we have the coasters. This next level is a group of people that, even if they didn't want to come to the training class (and you're not going to hold that against them because many people don't), they still got something out of it. They didn't want to be there, but they've learned some things that might actually improve them, and they took it to heart. They now know that there's a chance that they can improve themselves. This is your middle group, I call them the coasters.

Now, what's important about this middle group is even though they get a lot of good information that they admit they should put into place, they will go back to their jobs and not make a single change. They will not do anything differently. They will not change in any way. They will not actually apply any of the learned skills whatsoever. They will talk about how good it was. They will talk about how much it helped, but at the end of the day they will not make a single change.

This is very common, so don't be angry at these people, this is just who they are. This makes up the majority of the people that will attend a training class. The training class won't hurt them. It might help them a little bit because they have an increased understanding, but they still won't change anything they do. These are the people who get a lot of your work done at your company, so don't punish them.

THE IMPROVERS

Next are the improvers. The third and highest level is a group of people that, even if they didn't want to be at a training class (again, we forgive them because most people don't), they still got something out of it. They decided that something was worthwhile and that improvement was possible. And then, these people go back and change things while others don't. They actually try it. They put something into place and make some kind of change that they wouldn't have without the training.

These are the people that are on the highest level. They work to improve them-selves, because they see improvement as important and they embrace change. They hate failure, but not change. These are the people whom you want to focus on because these are going to ultimately be your top performers. These will be the people who do not resist change in your organization; they will almost always naturally rise to the top.

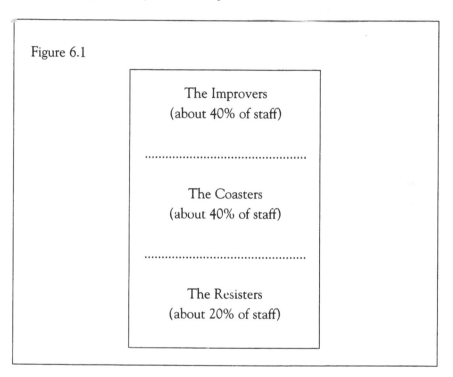

Figure 6.1

The Improvers
(about 40% of staff)

The Coasters
(about 40% of staff)

The Resisters
(about 20% of staff)

But of this group, there are actually two sub groups (See Figure 6.2). Notice the improvers are divided into two groups of people. The lower section of these two groups of people are the people who even if they didn't want to be in the class, they still got something out of it, they still got some value from it. They went back and changed something, but when it didn't work out perfectly, they quit. They didn't try it again. They tried it initially, sure enough, so they're much better than the people who didn't try it. (They're a whole lot better than the people that went around trying to convince other people not to try.) They actually did make a change. Yet when it didn't work out perfectly, they quit. They feel they have failed, and they don't like failure. They simply stopped and went back to their old ways. Now these are still the top level of your performers in your organization, but nevertheless, they will stop when it doesn't work out right. I call them the tryers.

THE ACHIEVERS

And finally, we have the top half of the top group. This usually makes up about 10% — maybe at the most 15% — of the people in your organization. These are the people you should spend all your time and money on; you want to spend all your effort on them. These are the people who will ultimately rise to the top of your organization, be your most effective leaders, they will facilitate change in your organization, and they will be the most productive people. You want to promote them, and spend all of your time with them. Who are they? They are the achievers.

These are the people that, even if they didn't want to come to class (and even the very top performers don't like going to training classes), they still got something out of it. They went back to their desks and attempted to make a change, and when it didn't work out perfectly, they just kept trying. They kept working at it; they didn't give up. They know that what they learned is valuable, and it's just a matter of time before they get it right. They're persistent in continuing to try to make it work. Their persistence is their outward expression that they believe in themselves, and they see it that way.

They will not give up on something that they believe has value; they will keep trying until it works. These are the people who will always rise to the top of an organization and always become leaders of the company. They help facilitate change in your organization. These are what I call the achievers. This is where you want to spend all your time and money, spend all your focus on these people. This is where all your attention deserves to be.

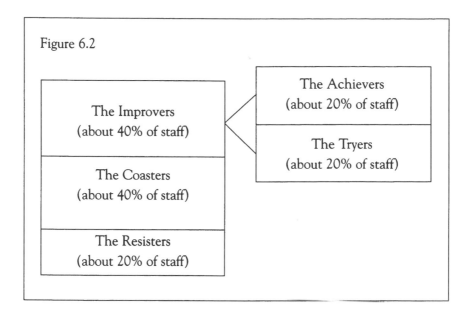

Figure 6.2

Now, after I finish this speech, of course, top management is always very excited. And their next response is "Well that's terrific! That's great, now we know who to spend our time and money on. That helps us quite a bit. Now all we have to do is decide who those people are." And I say, "Yep, that's all you have to do."

And they say, "So, how do we do that? Who gets to decide? How do we know who those people are?" And my response is, "Oh . . . you don't get to decide that."

Stunned, they then ask, "Then who does get to decide who these people are and where they fall?" And my response, as I point to the different types of people I just outlined is, "Well, they do. They get to decide. They're the ones who will make this decision, not you. No supervisor can take it away from them, and no manager can force them into it. They will make a conscious decision where they fall. They will make this decision. It is 100% in their control; it cannot be influenced by anybody."

"Each of these employees that you send to class will decide where they fall.

Your task is to send everybody, and simply watch where they decide they are. These people will make a decision about who they are and where they will ultimately end up. Their decision will be much more accurate than you can even hope to be. Everybody goes, and just let the chips fall where they may."

The reason I'm sharing this with you, the reader, at this stage, is because if you've gone through this book up to this point, you have an opportunity. You have an opportunity to decide where you fall. You have an opportunity to decide what type of person you want to be. I've tried as best I can to give you the clearest definition and dividing line that I can. By the time you finish this book, you will fall into one of the categories. You have to. It's time for you to decide where you fall, because you will make this decision. You now know it, and so does anybody who gave you this book.

Take this opportunity, before you finish this book, to decide where you fall.

THE POOR ADJUSTER (USUALLY A RESISTER OR A COASTER)

Some poor adjusters like training because it gets them away from their job that they hate. It also gives them an opportunity to complain about being at the class, complain about their work, and maybe even complain about their manager.

Most poor adjusters, however, really hate training classes. They would much rather complain about not getting enough training than to actually receive any. In fact, when one of these people makes a mistake, their response is to usually say, "Well nobody trained me to do it that way." Then, when you try to give them training, their response is, "Do I have to go?"

They also hate training because it makes it harder for them to complain that nothing will ever improve. That's why they are so busy running around telling everyone at break that nothing will ever work. They don't want it to work. They want everyone down at their level.

Whenever I see these people, I always remember what Paul Harvey once

100

said, "I have never seen a monument erected to a pessimist."

THE GOOD ADJUSTER (USUALLY A COASTER OR A TRYER)

The good adjusters don't fight training but accept it. When their manager or supervisor comes to them and tells them that they want them to go to a training class, or read training materials, or listen to tapes, that adjuster will do it. They won't argue. They will simply go to the training class, they'll learn what they can, and pretty much that's it. This is a nice person to have around because they don't fuss and fight. They're probably in that coasters level of people I was previously talking about. They didn't really want to go, but they certainly didn't put up a fight, and they actually got something out of it. This is the good adjuster.

THE EXCELLENT ADJUSTER (USUALLY A TRYER OR AN ACHIEVER)

The excellent adjuster will actually seek information. They'll look for self-improvement tapes; they'll look for classes about things that they could improve in. They'll actually contact local colleges to see if there are courses that would apply to them. They will seek the advice of a supervisor or a manager as far as what they can do to improve. They may spend time with the senior people in the office to try to get tips to improve. These are the people that know that they need to improve, and want to, and will take steps to do it. These are excellent adjusters.

THE AWESOME ADJUSTER (ALWAYS AN ACHIEVER)

The Awesome Adjusters, however, not only go out and seek information, but they're involved in giving the information to others. They will bring up information that they learned in an office meeting, and share it. They will review articles that have to do with some case law or policy wording and maybe even recap them and distribute them to other people. When they attend training sessions, they take notes and share the information with other people in their organization or unit.

Anyone who's been involved in any type of training knows that you tend to learn a subject much more rapidly when you're involved in having to explain it to other people. It heightens your ability to understand it, explain it and of course utilize it.

Awesome Adjusters, who develop themselves by using this approach, can usually develop in a few months what a good adjuster will take a year to do. This is simply because the learning process is so rapid for them.

Dave Vanderpan was a lot like that. Dave first worked for me as a claims supervisor. He would volunteer to organize passing on the information to the other team members. This meant putting on small training sessions, summarizing long legal updates, highlighting articles, and a number of other things. Dave was so good at putting on these little training sessions, that other managers would attend. In fact, they would even ask him to come to their offices to put on the training for their office. Quite a lot of responsibility for a claims guy who is just trying to better himself.

It backfired on Dave however. You see, he was so good that even after he went from claims supervisor, to claims manager, to regional claims manager, he was always asked to be involved in putting on training sessions. But there is a happy ending.

I am proud to say that today Dave is Director of Claims Training and Associate Dean of the School of Claims Performance at International Insurance Institute, Inc. He and I have developed many claims courses together, and he is widely considered one of the most dynamic and engaging instructors in the country. But once, he was a claims adjuster who never seemed to tire of learning new things, and liked being involved in helping others do the same thing.

CHAPTER 7

Customer Service / Empathy

I'm aware that there are thousands of books having to do with customer service in the marketplace. I would like to take a different approach to all the studies and the data that has been compiled and provide a real world approach based on my observations of the truly outstanding companies that I've had the opportunity to work with. In all of the training courses that I have conducted for companies, all of the work I have flow-charted, all of the interviews I have conducted with employees, all of the monitoring I've done of telephone conversations and reviewing of work productivity, I have found that the truly awesome customer service companies are the ones with employees that have two common characteristics.

The first one is that the employees, those in the position of providing customer service, can accurately describe their job. The second is that they understand what customer service is.

BEING ABLE TO ACCURATELY DESCRIBE YOUR JOB

Let's start this section with an exercise. If you are a claims person, this should apply to you. Go ahead and complete the exercise in Figure 7.1.

Figure 7.1

As a claims person, my job responsibilities are:

_____

_____

_____

_____

_____

_____

_____

Is Customer Service anywhere on your list? Providing customer service is really the only thing you needed to put down. If you put down things like "Pay claims," or "Investigate," or "Negotiate," or anything at all that focuses on tasks, then I want to tell you about a movie.

There's a movie by the name of "Clockwatchers" starring Parker Posey, Lisa Kudrow, Toni Collette, and Alanna Ubach. The opening scene is one of the funniest I can remember. It starts off by being a blank screen, and all you can hear is the ticking of a clock. The scene opens with a man sitting at a reception desk while a woman customer is standing there, facing him. The man who is behind the reception desk is reading a magazine, casually flipping through it, completely ignoring the woman who's standing right in front of him. We, the audience, continue to hear the clock ticking and are wondering what's going on until there's a close up on the clock. Sure enough, it's one minute to nine o'clock.

We continue to watch this man casually flipping through the magazine until the clock finally strikes exactly nine o'clock. The man puts away the magazine, folds his hands, looks up at the woman in front of him, smiles, and says, "Can I help you?"

I show this movie in my Awesome Claims Customer Service class. When I have the opportunity to discuss this with students, I will ask them, "Is this a good employee?" And the response always is "No." I'll ask, "Why not?" And the students will say something along the lines of, "Well, he ignored the customer" or "He should have helped her." My response is, "But, you don't know what his job is, so how can you pass judgment upon him?" And the replies I get are usually something like, "It doesn't matter what his job is, he still should have helped that person."

When I get to that stage of the discussion, I will usually ask, "Have you ever heard anybody say, 'I'm not going to do that, that's not my job?'" Of course most people will admit that not only have they heard that, but they have said that themselves. That's right, nobody likes doing anything that's not their job. This man probably should have helped that customer, but we don't know what his job is. Let's imagine what his job might be.

What if when he was hired, his manager sat down with him and described his job in detail. You see, the last person this manager had was always late and always left early, he missed some days from work, he wouldn't smile at customers, he wouldn't ask how he could help them. So this manager, in order to make sure that this new employee does an excellent job, gave him a set of job objectives.

The first job objective is that he would always be at work at nine o'clock. He started at nine o'clock and he should never be late. The second objective was to never leave early. The office shut down at five o'clock, and he was never to walk off even a minute early. Third, he had an hour for lunch and he was never to be late or, be gone for longer than an hour. Fourth, when he was to greet a customer, he was always to smile and look at the customer and ask, "How may I help you?" This manager made this person's job responsibilities very clear.

So now, let me ask you the reader, is this a good employee? Well, I don't know if he's a good employee, but I can tell you one thing. If those were his job objectives, he's doing his job. This guy is doing his job! He's doing exactly what he's been told his job is. True, he's not doing much more, but that's okay.

As a manager, I will take a person who does exactly what he thinks his job is, over someone who doesn't give a damn, any day of the week. All I have to do is take the person who does exactly what he thinks his job is and change his focus. All I have to do is to show this person that he's actually in the customer service business, and now he will do whatever it takes to be consistent with what he thinks his job is.

I'll bet this receptionist thinks he is an excellent employee. As a matter of fact, every three months when this guy sits down with his supervisor, his supervisor says, "Well, you were never late, and you never left early. You never took more than an hour for lunch. You always smile when you look at the customer; you always ask how you can help them. You are great; you did all your job objectives. Here's your raise."

As a matter of fact, this person's been getting raises this past year. On top of that, his co-workers come by and tell him how great he is. They say things like, "Oh, you're so much better than the last guy, he was always late, and you're never late." This person's getting nothing but positive feedback, so to say he's a bad employee, is just not fair. What this person needs is training, so he knows his job is bigger than his individual responsibilities. His job is to provide customer service, and he needs to understand that.

One of the hallmarks of great adjusters is that they understand what business they're in. Even if they don't work with the general public, they still have customers, be it their boss or co-workers, or maybe even vendors. Who knows? The point is in claims we have our customers, and we must understand that even though our tasks or our responsibilities might be listed out in detail, our overall job is to provide customer service to whoever our customer is. And the most Awesome Adjusters are the ones who always understand that and do whatever it takes to make sure they provide excellent customer service.

I was at a conference once, speaking on customer service in fact, when I realized I had forgotten to purchase some of the candy bars I like to hand out during my speech. I usually hand out candy bars to people who give me any kind of answer at all; I don't even care if it's right.

I went over to the bell desk and told a bellman I was about to perform my speech but I had forgotten to purchase some candy bars. I asked him if there was any way I could give him some money so he could run across the street and maybe purchase some candy bars and bring them to me. I was quite surprised when he said, "You know, I'm only supposed to carry the baggage in and out of the hotel."

I knew what he was saying. In his own words he was saying, "That's not my job." He didn't want to do it because it wasn't his job. He did not perceive himself as being in the customer service business. If you ask this person what his job is, he will probably tell you, "My job is to take the luggage out of the car, put it on the cart, take the cart to the front desk, wait for the customer to check in, take the cart up to their room and unload it." Then he might tell you after he receives his tip, his job is to go back down there and do it again. He might say that sometimes his job is to take luggage from a room and put it into a car. He might tell you his job is to put tags on luggage so it doesn't get confused with others. He might tell you a whole variety of other things.

What this person probably will not tell you is that his job is to provide customer service. He doesn't know that's his job; he thinks his job is to load luggage. When I asked him to do something to please a customer, his response was very consistent with what he believes his job is.

After being frustrated with that, I happened to be walking by the front desk and I gave the person there kind of an odd look that showed my frustration. He asked, "Can I help you, sir?" And I asked him (without telling him what had just happened to me), if there was any way I could get some help in getting some candy bars purchased for my presentation. He took the ten dollars out of my hand and said, "I'll bring them in as soon as I can."

I went to give my presentation, and about ten minutes after I began my presentation, in walked this gentleman, with a bag of candy bars and my change. He handed me the bag, but before he left I stopped him and pulled him up to the front of the room in front of 150 supervisors/managers who were there to see me speak. Since I was speaking on customer service, I thought this was appropriate.

I pointed out to the crowd the two scenarios. The first one was that the bellman wouldn't do something because it wasn't his job, and the second where this person was willing to do whatever it took to please the customer. Why did this happen? Very simple. The second person did not know that his job was to check people in. He did not know that his job was to sign time cards. He didn't know that his job was to make sure the beds were made before checking people in. This front desk person, for some reason, thought his job was to provide customer service. He understood he was in the customer service business, and because he understood his job was customer service, he did something that was completely consistent with providing customer service. He went and helped the customer do something that they needed done. His job was customer service and that's what he provided.

The bellman didn't know his job was customer service, and that's why he didn't help. And that's probably one of the most important dividing lines that there is between whether an adjuster will be an Awesome Adjuster or a good adjuster. Awesome Adjusters understand that they're in the customer service business. They need to provide customer service, and they understand that that means to do things outside of their job duties and descriptions.

Adjusters who hold themselves back by always trying to determine if something is "their job" usually falter and are frustrated by sometimes being forced to do something that they don't perceive they should be doing. It will only hurt them; it doesn't hurt anyone but themselves. They miss the opportunities to impress other people with how dedicated they are, and they place barriers in front of themselves to realizing their potential, simply because they don't want to be inconsistent with what they perceive their job is.

Awesome Adjusters don't have this problem. They know that their job is to provide outstanding customer service. Therefore, they're willing to do things consistent with that impression.

Another example: I was listening to a phone call in an insurance office when a claims adjuster received a call from Samay, an agent. The conversation goes like this:

Adjuster: *May I help you?*

Samay: *Yes, we faxed in a loss report and nobody's called the customer. What's going on?*

Adjuster: *I don't see it here on the list on my screen. Why don't you call the 800 number and report it?*

Samay: *We did that yesterday, and we were told that if we faxed it to you, it might get handled quicker. So what's up?*

Adjuster: *Well, it's not here on my screen, call the 800 number and report it and we'll get working on it right away.*

Samay: *Look, can't you take this loss?*

Adjuster: *Well, I can, but if you call the 800 number, they'll take your report and then send it right over.*

So let me ask a question, is this adjuster providing outstanding customer service? No. What should she be doing, if she knows how and she can (which she did)? I was listening to this conversation and I was thinking to myself, "Oh, for heaven's sake, just take this loss report. You're not making your job any easier because now all you're going to have is a pissed-off agent on your hands. Then you're still going to have to do the work, or someone else will have to deal with this agent and it will just make their job harder."

Why didn't this advisor take this loss report? Was she stupid? No, I talked to this girl. She was a pretty smart cookie. Was she lazy? No, she was working until six o'clock that night, she certainly wasn't lazy. So why didn't she take this loss report from this agent? Very simple, it's not her job.

You see, she's not in the customer service business as far as she knows. She thinks she's in the "Handle a claim once it's been reported" business. She's not in the customer service business, so she made a decision that was completely consistent with what she thinks her job is. Had she thought she was involved in the customer service business, she would have taken this loss report and handled the issue. She would have saved time for herself, or whoever else would have handled this claim, and impressed a customer in the meantime. The only reason that she didn't make the right decision is because she doesn't understand the business that she's in.

Now, we've had a brief discussion on the first criteria for outstanding customer service claims operations. Which is, that the people in the job can accurately describe their job. One of the things we train in the Awesome Claims Customer Service class is for adjusters to change their focus from what they thought they did as their job, by listing the tasks that they do, to describing their job correctly, which is providing customer service.

So let's look at the second criteria for great customer service for claims operations. That is, the people who are charged with the responsibility of providing customer service — everyone in claims — understand exactly what customer service is.

WHAT IS CUSTOMER SERVICE?

What I'd like you to do at this time is to get out a piece of paper and finish this sentence, "Customer service is _____." Go ahead and write anything you want, it can be a sentence, it can be a list, it can be a picture. Doesn't matter. What I want is for you to define what customer service is, and when you're finished, go ahead and turn the page.

See Figure 7.2. This is usually the list or the descriptions I receive when I ask adjusters in training classes to define customer services. Are any of the items you put down on this list? If so, then that means you're one of the gang and you probably did a pretty good job.

Figure 7.2

Customer Service is . . .

Being patient
Listening
Service with a smile
Doing for others as you would like them to do for you
Making the customer satisfied
Answering questions
Doing what you say you're going to do
Paying claims
Going beyond the call of duty
Following through
Returning phone calls

However, what's missing from Figure 7.2 is the main criteria that I have found for customer service. My personal observations in dealing with companies that provide outstanding claims customer service is that the claims people understand that customer service is meeting or exceeding a customer's expectations. And that is true regardless of what the expectation is.

Everyone knows that there are some customers, that no matter what you do, you can't please. But there are also customers where we fumble every step of the claims process, and they're still happy. Why? Because they don't know any better. Their expectations are low, or they don't have any, so anything we do for them is fine. Sometimes we get the customer service wins when we don't deserve them, and sometimes we get the customer service losses when we don't deserve them.

The criteria, however, is exactly the same: if you meet or exceed the customer's expectations, you have a customer service win, and you'll probably hold on to that person as a customer. If you fall short of those expectations, whatever they are, you'll probably ultimately lose that customer.

The key here, is that in claims, we have the opportunity to set those expectations. Awesome Adjusters understand that great customer service is meeting or exceeding customers' expectations and having the talent and the skill to set those expectations. That way they can make sure they exceed them.

Let me give you an example: I was listening to a phone call in a claims office, when Layne, the customer, called in and got Molly, the adjuster, and the conversation went just like this:

Molly: *Can I help you?*

Layne: *Yeah, I'm having a real problem with the body shop you guys sent me to; they keep saying that they're ordering the right parts but the car's not getting delivered on time. They're saying that I have to pay for an extra part because it's not included in the estimate, and I am really upset. They're saying that you guys told them you weren't going to pay for the part and my car can't get fixed without it.*

Molly: *Do you know what part it is?*

Layne: *No, I don't know the name of the part. I'm really frustrated.*

Molly: *Okay, let me call the body shop and then I'll call you right back.*

Layne: *Fine, thanks.*

Now let me ask you, the reader, right now, what is the expectation of when Layne will get a call back? When does Layne expect to get this return phone call? Is it one minute, is it two, is it five minutes, is it 20 minutes, how long? Guess what, we don't know. We don't have the foggiest idea of what Layne's expectation is of when she's going to get a call back, and yet it is the only criteria for whether or not we provide great customer service.

So, let's continue on with what happened. Molly calls the body shop and it takes the body shop person a good 15 minutes just to get to the phone. Then he has to go out and look at the car, come back, and they had to talk for another 15 minutes. Then the body shop guy had to call the parts distributor to get some prices and that took another five minutes. All in all this call took about 35 minutes.

In my opinion Molly did a fantastic job. Any less trained, any less experienced, and Molly would have gotten snookered. But she didn't. She walked this body shop guy through every single step of the repair process, which showed that the parts that he was talking about were actually included in the prices that they had already paid. By the time Molly was done, the body shop person admitted that he was wrong and Molly was right, and that they would go ahead with the repairs as outlined. Of course at this point in monitoring this phone call I thought that Molly had done an incredible job.

Molly gets back on the phone, calls Layne, and guess what Layne said. That's right! She said, "What took you so long?"

Molly's response was to try to explain to Layne why it took so long. She explained about the body shop guy looking at the car and calling the parts place. But of course all that did was irritate Layne because now it only sounds like a bunch of excuses. When Molly tried to explain that this was done in a very short period of time, Layne just got even more irritated and said, "Hell, if I knew it was going to take this long, I would have told you to call me at work!"

They argued for a few more minutes, and then Molly finally told Layne, "By the way, I did solve the problem." And Layne's reply was, "Yeah, fine, whatever." And then she hung up.

Let me ask this question: what were these two people talking about? Were they talking about the great job that Molly had just done for Layne? Were they talking about the great customer service that Molly provided? No, they were talking about the fact that Layne's expectations were not met. Even though Molly did a fantastic job technically, she did not use the most important tool that she has at her disposal, to provide outstanding customer service; that is to set the expectations of the customer so she can meet or exceed them.

What if (and I'm just proposing this), instead of saying "I'll call you right back," Molly would have said, "Okay, I'll tell you what. I'll call the body shop. It could easily take the body shop person a good half hour, maybe an hour to take a look at the car and to review it. He and I will have to talk about it which could easily take another fifteen minutes, and we might even have to call the person who wrote the estimate. That could easily take another fifteen minutes. This whole process could easily take an hour and a half. It's 9:00 now, what if I call you back by 10:30?" And then Layne might reply, "Fine, then call me at work."

After calling the body shop, now, we call Layne back at 9:30 at work, with the answer. Have we met this person's expectations? Yes, as a matter of fact, we've exceeded them. The only difference between the first interaction and the second interaction is that we took the time to set Layne's expectations in the first place.

Awesome Adjusters know that great customer service is meeting or exceeding customer expectations and, most importantly, taking the opportunity to set those expectations when it's possible.

THE CLAIMS CUSTOMER SERVICE STATEMENT

When meeting with top management at insurance companies that wish to improve customer service, I usually ask them what their claims customer service statement is. Invariably, most companies don't have a separate customer service statement for claims. I'm a strong believer that claims needs a customer service statement for itself.

Very often, insurance companies are divided up into two groups. There's claims, and then there is everybody who is not in claims. In any insurance company, claims operations tend to be an island unto themselves. I'm not saying it's right, but I am saying claims is in a completely different world than the rest of the company. For that reason, claims operations need a customer service statement.

A customer service statement is not a mission statement. It's not a goal to be achieved ultimately. A customer service statement is a statement that the claims people can hold true to how they want to do their jobs. It is a philosophy of sorts, kind of a guiding principle that tells anyone who wants to know how it is, as claims people, we'd like to do our jobs.

I've worked with many different insurance companies trying to develop good customer service statements. My favorite was this:

We understand that accidents can be upsetting and unwelcome circumstances for our customers. Our goal is to fairly and accurately resolve the claim in a timely manner with our customers as our partners.

Well, that smells pretty sweet, doesn't it? I'm all warm and fuzzy, how about you? It's a pretty good statement, don't you think?

But do we? Do we understand that accidents can be upsetting and unwelcome circumstances for our customers? Do we really understand this? Most claims adjusters will say that they certainly understand this to be true. However, I hardly hear it anywhere. I hardly actually hear an adjuster, in a conversation that I'm monitoring, demonstrate that the customer has been through something difficult and unwanted.

I do hear the claims adjuster tell the customer that they have to sign a form or else they won't get paid. I hear adjusters tell customers they are going to have to get an estimate or there's nothing that can be done. However, I rarely hear a claims adjuster demonstrate that he understands that the customer's been through an upsetting situation. I'm not saying that it's not being done, I'm simply saying that in all my monitoring, I almost never hear it.

Let me ask you, the reader, this question. In a year's worth of monitoring phone calls all over the country with all different insurance companies, as you can imagine, I hear some pretty upset people. There is no way you can listen to claims calls all day long and not hear some very upset people on the phone. How many times, in the last year, do you imagine I heard any claims person say to any customer something like this, "You know I am sorry that this happened to you," or "I know this is difficult for you, and I am going to try to help you because I understand that," or "I know you didn't ask for this, and I know this will be tough, but I will help you the best I can," or anything even remotely similar to those three sentences? How many times do you think I heard this in the last year?

Well, for those of you claims people that believe customer service is a part of your job, you can imagine it being heard a lot. For most of us, we will probably imagine that I didn't hear it very often. In fact, in the last calendar year of monitoring phone calls, I only heard a comment like this one time. Again, I am not saying that it is not being done, I am simply saying I almost never hear it.

If we understand that accidents can be upsetting and unwelcome circumstances for our customers, who is telling the customers we understand it? Who is actually telling them that we understand what they are going through? Is anyone? The Awesome Adjuster, that's who.

Remember the guy who referred to himself as being the victim? When our only response to this person, who is feeling like a victim, is to tell him what will happen to him if he doesn't cooperate with us, it doesn't sound too much like we understand this is a difficult process for him.

How about that second statement about our customers as our partners? Well as we learned before, we have a very important tool called the hammer. We tend to bring out the hammer quite a bit, and we can't wait to use it every chance we get. The idea of treating customers as partners is to simply let them know that we will do our best to help them whenever we can and to point out how we will help them if they cooperate instead of what we will do to them if they don't.

CUSTOMER SERVICE STANDARDS

Basically there are five customer service standards in the area of claims. Awesome Adjusters know them and practice them.

They are:
1. Explanation of the process
2. Empathy
3. Prompt and Equitable Settlements
4. Keeping Promises
5. Meeting and Exceeding Expectations

EXPLANATION OF THE PROCESS

We all know that customers are entitled to know what's going to happen to them. They are entitled to know what steps we are going to take and how long they should take. Most of the time we do a pretty good job of explaining to people what's going to happen to them; unfortunately we explain it to them in a way that sounds more like they are going to get run over by a steamroller. We tell them what they are going to have to do, when they are going to have to do it, and what will happen to them if they don't.

Excellent customer service is explaining the process in a way that makes the customer feel that we're on their side, or that we're going to try to help them. This is even true of a claimant who's completely at fault. Even if the process is going to point out that he's at fault for the accident, we can still treat him with respect and be knowledgeable and fair-minded about the process.

EMPATHY

There's that word again, empathy. I hear it get thrown around a lot in claims discussions and office meetings, but like I said before, I rarely hear anybody providing any empathy. Not never . . . but rarely.

I was with this one company which didn't have the ability to monitor phone calls so I had to sit next to the person and listen on an extension. I was listening to a loss report taker getting calls when this one woman calls in very upset. She'd already called in to give part of the loss to another loss report

118

taker, but she had to leave for some reason. Now she was calling in to finish giving the loss to someone else and was frustrated that this new person didn't have all the information.

The new loss report taker did her best job and she started asking the lady, "Madam, do you know where your car is?" And she responded quite angrily, "Yes, of course I know where my car is. It's sitting out in front of my yard. It's smashed. It's wrecked. I can't even drive it!"

The loss report taker tried to calm her down by saying, "Okay, madam, that's fine, that's fine, are you injured?" The lady's response was, "Well of course I'm injured! I've got a cut running down my arm for crying out loud. I already told the other lady this. What's wrong with you?" The loss report taker responded with, "Okay, madam, that's fine, now where can we take a look at you car?"

This went on and on for about five minutes and finally the loss report taker said, "Okay, madam, we'll try to get someone out there as soon as we can. Just wait for the adjuster to call and I'll try to get someone to call you as soon as possible." The loss report taker hangs up the phone, turns to me, and says, "God! What was her problem?"

What was her problem? That was the question this loss report taker wanted to know. What was this lady's problem? It's almost like she was asking, "What's wrong with this lady, Carl, why was she acting like that? Do you think she had a bad childhood? Do you think she had some kind of mental disease? What's this lady's problem, Carl?"

As soon as I heard her ask this question, I realized that empathy was not part of this loss report taker's philosophy. She was projecting on to this lady how she thought this lady should have treated her. She wasn't providing empathy at all, even though if you ask her, she'll say she did. Empathy is understanding where people are coming from; it is understanding that they have pain. It is not taking on the pain, such as sympathy. But it is simply understanding where the pain's coming from and that they have it.

What was this lady's problem? I know what this lady's problem was. She'd been involved in an auto accident. She was scared out her mind for crying out loud. This lady was shaken, upset, and she was yelling and screaming at someone who didn't deserve it at all. But that's what people do when they get upset. And when this loss report taker asked me what her problem was, I knew that there was some room to grow in the area of empathy.

Most of us in claims will state that a big part of our job is to provide empathy. I just never hear it. Whenever I ask a group of claims people in a customer service class when they provide empathy, I normally get back something like, "when there's blood," or "when there's a serious injury," or "when there's a total loss," or "when there's a fatality." Usually something along those lines.

We tend to empathize with people when, if we put ourselves in their place it would rattle us. If it would shake us up a bit to be going through what they are going through, then that's the point when we start to provide empathy. But, what happens to that criteria the longer you've been in claims? That's right, you start to become desensitized.

I heard a conversation in a claims office where one claims adjuster had come up to another claims adjuster and said, "Hey, did you hear about that claimant? Our insured ran right into him and cut his head right off, and it rolled right down the road, man." And the other adjuster replied, "Yeah, how far did it roll?"

That response isn't to show that we can be callous, or mean, or anything like that at all. It simply shows that after a while, when you've been in this business long enough, you can accept some pretty nasty things. I don't know if anybody could say anything to me, after this many years in the business, that would even raise my blood pressure. But even to a person whose fender got scratched, this is still someone who has to pay $500 that doesn't have $500 extra this month. This is still a guy who's got to figure out how he's going to get his kid to the day care center for three days without his car. This can still be a traumatic and unfamiliar event to this person. It doesn't mean all customers are upset, it just means that we as claims people have to remember that they all have the potential for being upset, regardless of the size of the claim.

DELIVERING ON PROMISES

I would say that most claims people are truly outstanding at delivering on promises . . . when they know they've made one. Problems arise sometimes because we as claims people are always making promises that we don't realize. We might say something like, "Okay, Mr. Jones, I'll call you back when we get the estimate." What we don't realize, is that we've actually made some kind of promise to this person. We don't know what it is, but this person has some kind of expectation of when we're going to call them. And then when we don't call them in two days, since this customer doesn't know how long it's going to take, he calls us, thinking we broke our promise.

The key is to make sure that we understand when we are making promises, and that means being specific about when we're going to call them. So perhaps we could've said, "Mr. Jones, I'll call you when the estimate comes in, it should take about three days. Since today's Monday, I should definitely call you by Friday." Now there's a chance that we can deliver on the promise of calling him when the estimate comes in and he will understand that we've kept our promise.

MEETING OR EXCEEDING EXPECTATIONS

As we stated before, the main characteristic of an outstanding customer service company is that they understand what customer service is. Customer service is meeting or exceeding the customer's expectations. It is one of the five standards of customer service as well. But there's an additional point to this expectation I'd like to add.

Let's say I have a claims adjuster by the name of John, and I'm his supervisor. One day I walk up to John and I say to him, "Hey, John, you're going to be getting a call in a little bit. It's going to be the most important call you will ever receive. In fact, in your entire career, here at this company, you will never receive a call from a more important customer than this person. So heads up."

In a few minutes, John gets a call. Are you going to see a change in John? Is he going to do something different than he did before? Yes, he will. John might pay a little bit more attention. If the person expresses frustration or anger, he might actually apologize and show empathy. Would John make a phone call, even if it's not his job, if it would help the claims process go more smoothly? The answer is, yes, of course he would. In fact, John's going to make a lot of decisions about what to do in light of who he thinks this customer is.

Here's my point. Anything you see John change in his process, because he thinks he knows who's calling, is an opportunity for improvement. Anything you can imagine John changing because of what he knows is an opportunity for improvement in your office. It means we could change if we wanted to, we just don't want to. And the reason we don't want to is because we believe it would take too much time. The truth, however is that many things that we would change if we thought we would be dealing with the most important customer we ever had to deal with, would actually save us time. We just don't recognize it.

The idea isn't to run around treating every single customer like they're the most important customer. That's not possible anyway, and it would just wear us out. The idea here is that if we would be willing to change some things for the most important customer we ever had, and those things will make our job easier, then why not do it for all of our customers?

THE NAME CALLING PARADOX

Whenever I visit a claims office, it doesn't take too long before I hear someone get upset over a conversation they are having, hang up the phone, and exclaim, "Damn that idiot, what a jerk!"

As claims people we all know we have tough customers whom we have to deal with, and when things get really difficult, we love to hang up the phone, walk around, and tell everyone else how badly we've been treated. We just can't wait to go around and tell all of our buddies in the office what an idiot, jerk, or moron we've just had to deal with.

I was in a claims office one time when an adjuster was walking around the office with a Dictaphone because he had just taken a recorded statement. He was walking around the office saying to everyone, "Hey, you wouldn't believe the idiot I just talked to, listen to this."

We are very quick in claims to huddle together and tell stories about some idiot, jerk, or moron. In fact, as I mentioned, it doesn't take but a couple of hours in any claims office anywhere in the country before I start to hear this type of terminology referred to when speaking about customers who have made us upset.

I realize that, of course, we do this to blow off steam. But the underlying damage is often hard to see. In fact, what I'm going to point out in this next section is that, if in any way you believe that a company can deliver outstanding customer service while that stuff is going on, then I need to completely change your point of view in a short period of time.

We all know that we have to deal with difficult customers. People get upset because they're in a process that they don't like, didn't ask for, and sometimes have to pay a price for the honor of being involved. We are not travel agents, and we are not booking people on a cruise. We're not selling some product out of a department store. We deal with people when they've had an upsetting, unwelcome event happen to them that they didn't like and didn't ask for.

People often times can get upset, and we should understand that. However, you know that there are times when our reaction is going to be to hang up the phone and call them names. Because we believe it helps us blow off steam.

Most customer service experts, however, would point out that is completely inconsistent. You cannot be a great customer service company while the people who are in charge of delivering the customer service are free to run around

123

calling the customers names.

What's worse, in claims, is that this is often condoned by the management team. In fact, it won't take any time at all before I hear an adjuster come up to a manager and say, "You won't believe what this idiot just told me." Usually, the adjuster is not corrected in any way, and the manager just continues on to try to find out what the customer said. This is damaging beyond belief. This is a totally destructive interaction that destroys all hopes of the insurance industry ever delivering outstanding customer service.

Now before I continue on my soap box, let me just admit that I was the worst of the offenders. In fact, when I was a claims adjuster my favorite thing to do was to run around the office and tell everybody what an idiot I had just talked to. I'd run over to Ken and say, "Hey, Ken, you wouldn't believe what this jerk just said to me!" And if it was a good one, I'd gather my friends up together and say, "Hey you guys, let's go to break, I've got a good one for you; this one you're going to love." I'd tell my story and we'd all just laugh and have a great time.

My favorite target was my supervisor, let's call him Steve. I just loved to go to Steve and tell him all the dumb things that people used to say to me. I'd run over to Steve and say, "Hey, Steve, you wouldn't believe what this jerk just told me." And Steve would say, "Yeah, what'd the jerk say, Carl?" I'd tell him and we'd just laugh and laugh. It was a great bonding experience.

This went on for quite a while, almost three years, until one day, I got a new supervisor. Let's call him Doug. And Doug, I'll tell you, didn't think anything was funny. I thought for sure he just had no sense of humor whatsoever. I'd tell him the funniest stories and not a laugh would come out of his mouth. Until one day, I finally got a call that I thought would sure make Doug giggle just a little bit.

I had just settled a total loss Corvette with a claimant. Now, keep in mind this was a brand new Corvette and a very high priced vehicle. I had finished all of the negotiations and settled what I thought was a fair amount. Although it took awhile, we came to an agreement. Then, fifteen minutes later, this claimant called up and said, "Mr. Van, I just put a tank of gas into that car before it got in the accident, which I just thought of. Am I going to get paid for that tank of gas?"

I thought for sure that this was the dumbest thing I'd ever heard. A tank of gas after he had just been paid for an entire Corvette, a brand new Corvette at that. So of course, I ran over to Doug with my story, giggling to myself, just knowing that this was finally going to be the one that broke that first smile for Doug.

I ran over to Doug and said, "Doug! Doug! You wouldn't believe what this moron just said." Doug looked at me, paused for a moment and finally said, "Okay, Carl, congratulations. Great work. You caught somebody saying something stupid in a claim. Great job. Big wow. Now, Carl, now that you've done this fantastic thing, what are you going to do to help this guy?"

My reply was simple. "Help him? Help him do what? Pull his head out?"

Doug said, "No, Carl, help him understand that we're doing the right thing. Help this guy understand that we've paid him what he's entitled to get, and that he doesn't need to feel that he's been slighted. Help this guy believe that although he's been put in a bad situation, we've done the right thing and he's been treated fairly. Carl, if this guy feels so bad, if he feels so out of control, if he feels so violated, that a tank of gas is going to make him feel whole, then maybe he doesn't need you making fun of him behind his back. Maybe he just needs some help."

That was like a ton of bricks landing on my head. This was my favorite activity, after all. I just loved to run around the office telling people what idiots I'd just talked to. And now, with a few comments, my whole world came crashing down on top of me.

I'm ashamed to admit it, but I was a claims adjuster for three years before anybody had ever referred to my job as helping people. Nobody had ever referred to my job, in any way, as helping people. It was nowhere in my objectives, there was not one word about it in any of my reviews to that point. Nobody had used the words "help people" as part of my job.

This had a profound effect on me. Why? Because I liked to help people. I don't drive up and down the highway looking for people with flat tires. But if someone came to me and said, "Hey, can you give me a jump because my battery is dead?" I'd say yes. I don't run around looking for people to help, but I do like helping people when I can. When my supervisor referred to my job as helping people, it turned my head completely around.

Once I realized my job was to help people, even if they were complaining, even if they were bitching, even if they were angry, even if they were doing things that people tend to do when they are in a situation that they don't like, don't want, didn't ask for, if I could keep my head, and treat that person with respect, I'd actually be helping him. And once I realized my job was to help people, my job became so much easier.

Let me say that again. Once I realized my job was to help people, my job became much, much easier. I found it much easier to be patient, I found it much easier to be helpful, and I found it much easier to deal with people when they're upset and angry and even accusatory and attacking. I found it much easier to do my job, which was to do whatever it takes to help him by making sure the claim goes smoothly.

The idea here is that we deal with people when they're upset. We deal with people who are in a situation that they didn't want to be in, and they didn't ask for. Yet, when they act in a way that's perfectly consistent with what they've experienced, their big reward is to be called names, behind their backs, by the very people who are charged with delivering excellent customer service.

We, as claims folks, the very people who said that we understand that our customer has been through a traumatic, unfamiliar, unwanted events, the very people who understand that they're in a business of dealing with people who are in situations they didn't want, we are the ones calling customers names behind their backs. The idea that we could deliver, in claims, outstanding customer service while we, in claims, are free to call our customers names behind their backs, is so ludicrous, it's almost impossible to describe in words.

Often times, I will get comments back from people when I tell them this information, that there really are jerks out there, and there is no excuse for their behavior. I am told customers should understand that we are trying to help them, and we don't deserve to get yelled at or complained to, or lied to, or all of the things that sometimes customers do that make us angry at them. And I guess that's true. But I want to share a quick story with you that actually happened to me. You tell me if you think this guy is a jerk.

NO JUICE FOR YOU!

As I mentioned before, I fly frequently. I travel to a different city, sometimes two cities, every single week. That often involves taking four or five, maybe even six different individual planes in a week. In any given year I could easily fly on 200 to 250 planes. This gives me a great insight into the process of the airline industry, the rules and regulations, and of course the tricks, that most people wouldn't be aware of. Therefore, there's not too much that can happen in the process of taking a flight that can get me too upset, because I'm just so used to it.

One day I was sitting on an airplane near the front row, because I had been able to upgrade, when on walked a gentleman. Actually, it was an angry man. He walked up to the flight attendant who was standing right near the cockpit door, leaned over at her and screamed, "Where should I sit?" and shoved his airline ticket right in her face. Now keep in mind, this guy was about six foot two and weighed about 250 pounds. This flight attendant, we'll call her Susan, looked like she was about five foot four and weighed about 110 pounds. So when he leaned over and blasted at her, it shook her to her core.

Having just been screamed at, she looked up at the man and yelled back, "Well, how should I know where you're going to sit?"

127

He replied, "This is your plane isn't it? Don't you know where people sit? Are you that disorganized?"

She said, "Well, sir, I don't know where every single person on the plane sits, what does your ticket say?"

He yells, "It says 11 E."

"Well," she continued, "it's probably right down there past 10 E. Why don't you go have a seat?"

And he replied, "I will." Then he went stomping down the plane to go take his seat.

Right then, I could see it in her eyes. She looked over at me and rolled her eyes as if to say, "Oh, what a jerk." This guy walked on the plane and was yelling and screaming at some poor flight attendant who didn't do anything to him, and she fought back. Her reaction was perfectly normal given the circumstances.

So, was this guy a jerk? Well if you said yes, just remember you passed judgment on this guy. You said he's a jerk because of the way he acted, and that's fine. That flight attendant thought the same thing. She thought this guy was a jerk for yelling at her when he had no right to, and she decided she wasn't going to take it. So she fought back, and they got into a big battle, and then he stomped down the plane. She had the right to be upset at him for doing what he did and her reaction was perfectly normal.

Of course, then she got on the intercom and started yelling through the intercom, "EVERYONE MUST BE SEATED IN THEIR SEAT AT THIS TIME. WE CANNOT PULL AWAY FROM THE GATE UNLESS EVERYONE IS SEATED IN THEIR SEAT!"

Now, I know that she was actually yelling at him because I saw what happened, the problem was that everyone else on the plane was getting yelled at because she was mad at this one guy.

Then, she turns to her coworker off to her side and says, "See that guy down in 11 E? He's a real jerk. Don't give him any orange juice."

So now, she's going to play the old "Orange Juice Deprivation Trick" on the guy. That's right, because this guy acted like a jerk, he's now not going to get any orange juice. Again, this flight attendant's reaction was perfectly normal, to fight back with him, to yell at all of us, and now this poor guy's not going to get any orange juice because he acted in a way that was inconsistent with how she thought he should be behaving.

All this is perfectly reasonable. But let me tell you, her reaction would not have been the same had she seen what I saw. Had she seen what had happened 35 minutes before the guy had gotten on the plane like I did, this would not have been her reaction. What happened? Funny you should ask.

This guy had come to the airport to go on vacation. He dropped his wife and his little girl off while he went to park the car. His little girl is two, maybe three years old. He goes to park the car and in the meantime his wife and daughter run up to the gate. The flight attendants let the wife and daughter on the plane. Meanwhile, after parking the car, this guy goes down to the ticket counter and waits in the long line down there. He finally waits in line long enough to the point where when he gets up to the ticket counter, they tell him that he has to run up to the gate because the flight is about to leave.

He comes sprinting down the terminal, runs right up to the ticket counter and said, "I've got to get on this flight, I have a ticket and my wife and daughter are on the plane." The gate attendant said, "Sir, the plane's all full." And he replied, "But I've got to get on the plane, I've got my ticket right here." And the gate attendant said, "Well, sir, we had to give away your seat."

Stunned, he asks, "Give away my seat, how could you possibly give away my seat, I've got a ticket right here?" Her answer was, "Well, sir you've got to be here 15 minutes before the flight leaves." Stunned, he responded, "Well how the hell am I supposed to know that?" And she says, "Well, sir, it's right here on this ticket, you've got to be here 15 minutes before the flight leaves, now this really isn't our fault."

"But I've got to get on the plane!"

And she said, "Well, sir, this isn't our fault, you were supposed to be here fifteen minutes before the flight takes off."

Now, keep in mind, every time this attendant kept saying, "This isn't our fault," what is she really saying? That's right, she's really saying, "This is your fault."

So this went on and on while he demanded to get on the plane and they kept telling him that this wasn't their fault. Now, you should know, that this is a holiday weekend and Monday is a holiday. Right now it's Friday afternoon and Monday is a holiday, so every plane is booked solid. She finally said to him, "Well, sir, there's only one seat tomorrow, so what you can do, is you can let your wife and daughter go ahead and fly on, and you fly out the next day and catch up to them."

And he rejected that by explaining, "I can't do that, my wife doesn't even know where we're staying, I've got all the credit cards and all of the flight information, I've got to get on the plane."

So she says, "Well, sir, there are no seats because we gave it away, we can pull your wife and daughter off the plane and you can try to find a flight tomorrow, but there's only one seat available tomorrow, that means you won't be able to fly out until Sunday."

So he rambles, "But I've got to fly out today because we're leaving on our cruise and we've got to be there and we'll lose our whole cruise if we don't get out there tomorrow."

Getting frustrated, she explains, "Sir, this wasn't our fault, you should've been here 15 minutes before the flight, there's nothing we can do, there's just no seat available, there's only one seat and that's tomorrow. So either you fly tomorrow, or you let your wife fly tomorrow, but one of you is going to have to fly by yourself tomorrow."

And he says, "I can't do that! I've absolutely got to get on this flight, our whole vacation's going to be ruined if I don't get on this flight." So she says, "Sir, this isn't our fault, you should've been here 15 minutes before."

Now, this went on for about 15 to 20 minutes and he was getting more and more upset every time she told him this wasn't their fault. Now keep in mind, one of the reasons he stayed down at the ticket counter for half an hour is because the airline was so understaffed that people were waiting in line a half hour just to find out they were in the wrong spot. We in America have become so accustomed to absolutely horrible service from the airlines that we actually accept that it's okay to stand in line for hours because they don't want to properly staff their departments.

After about 20 minutes, this gate agent gets so upset with this guy, she finally turns to a coworker and says, "Alice, can you take care of this guy?" Alice walks over and the whole process starts all over again. Now keep in mind this was going on for about 30 minutes or so. Another thing to keep in mind is, even though the flight was delayed, they gave away his seat when he wasn't there within 15 minutes of the scheduled flight time, because they had people flying "Stand-By" and they wanted to put those people on the plane. The airline is manipulating its own rule because he was actually there 15 minutes before the flight took off. And that's because the flight was late.

After a while, it finally dawns on this guy that this is going to happen. He does realize that he's not getting on the plane, and his wife and daughter really are going to fly without him. And I'll tell you, just the thought, the mere thought, that his wife and daughter were going to be off in some city, alone, without him, was shaking this guy to the core so badly I thought he was going to break down and cry right there at the counter. He was holding onto the edge of the counter with his fist so tightly I could see the veins bulging out of his arms.

131

This guy was in utter pain. He was in excruciating pain, and the reward he got for using this airline was being told that none of this was their fault and basically he was at fault.

So after about 30 minutes of watching this, I finally got on the plane at the last minute like I like to do. I sit down in my seat, just sitting there for a couple of seconds, feeling very sorry for this person, when all of a sudden, who walks on the plane? This guy. That's right, this furious person out there, walked on the plane. Somehow he got a ticket. I don't know how it happened. Some miracle of miracles happened and somehow this guy got a ticket. I have no idea what happened, all I know is there he is getting on the plane.

He walks over to this flight attendant, this poor flight attendant who never did anything to him in his life, and he blasts at her about where he should sit. She feels that he shouldn't be talking to her that way, and she fights back, and they get in a big argument, and now this guy isn't going to get any orange juice.

That flight attendant's response of getting angry because of the way she got treated and fighting back by yelling at him, yelling at all of us, and depriving this poor guy of orange juice, is all perfectly normal, given the situation.

But let me submit this. This would not have been her reaction had she seen what I saw. If she had seen what this guy had gone through up there at the ticket counter, this would not have been her reaction. Any person with any "human compassion" bones in their body would not have fought this guy. Anybody who had seen what I saw, when confronted with this guy yelling at them about where he should sit, instead of fighting back, would have said, "Sir, I'm so sorry what you just went through, I saw what happened, and I'm terribly sorry. You are seated in 11E, let me show you to your seat."

In fact, one might even think we would continue on by saying, "Let me see if we can get your wife and your daughter to sit next to you." Maybe even, "Let me buy you a drink" (that way he'll be angry and drunk).

132

I'm not sure what any of us would say in this situation, had we seen what happened, but my guess is, had we actually seen what this person had gone through, our reaction would not have been to fight back, get angry, yell, and retaliate. Sadly enough, this flight attendant didn't see any of that. She was just minding her own business, and this guy came on yelling and screaming.

Was this guy a jerk? I really don't know. I do know one thing, that this guy was in a process that he didn't understand, he didn't have control over, and he felt he was being victimized. He felt he was being pushed around and it was out of control and all he kept getting was that this was his fault.

Was this guy a jerk? I don't know. I know he was a man who was frantic about being on the plane with his wife and daughter so he didn't lose a week's vacation. I know he was a guy who was upset at even the thought of leaving his wife and daughter to fend for themselves while he sat there. I know he was a guy in pain from being dragged through something he didn't like and didn't ask for. I know he was a guy that could have used some help.

The point of this story is that we get people like this in claims. We get people who are angry, we get people who are upset, we get people who say things they shouldn't say, we get people who sometimes lie or exaggerate or demand things even they know they are not entitled to. These are all perfectly normal things that some people do when they are involved in a process that they don't like, didn't want, and didn't ask for. They get pushed into something, and, unfortunately, we're not there to see the pain that they go through.

All we get is the reaction to the whole situation. Unfortunately, often times that reaction is for them to act in a way that's perfectly normal considering the circumstances. Sometimes they react by attacking us, and lying to us, and exaggerating, and demanding things out of us that they are not entitled to. These are all things that human beings do when they are involved in a painful situation.

The sad part, however, is that their big reward for coming to us as claims people, is to be called names behind their backs by the very people who promised that they would try to help them. Once again, the idea that we can run around calling customers names behind their backs, when they act in a way that's perfectly normal given their circumstances, and yet still call ourselves an outstanding customer service business, is preposterous. We will never achieve greatness as a customer service industry while that crap is going on. It's completely inconsistent with delivering great customer service.

Sure, we can deliver good customer service compared to other insurance companies, but that doesn't make us any good. That doesn't make us outstanding. That just means we are not as horrible as the next company that's doing the same thing. We will never achieve greatness in the area of customer service while we in the claims business are free to call customers names behind their backs. I do not believe that any great customer service company does this.

Take any great customer service company you can think of, American Express, Disney, or any company that you consider delivering great customer service. I don't believe that anyone in management is telling their employees that it is okay to call their customers names.

I don't believe that there is any manager at Disney, walking around telling their employees it's okay to call their customers idiots, jerks, and morons. And they're just trying to put people on a ride. We, on the other hand, are trying to help people who have been through a traumatic, unfamiliar, unwanted event.

As a customer service business, in a customer service environment, where our customers have been through something very difficult, unwanted, and unasked for, we should be extraordinarily empathetic to their plight, not more demanding. Most customers who find themselves in a claims situation and are responding negatively, have already been through a lot of pain. They are already in a situation that's causing them to react that way. They don't need any more pain out of us.

We in claims are in the business of dealing with human suffering. Yet often times we are trained to ignore it. I propose Awesome Adjusters do the opposite. Awesome Adjusters know that their jobs become much easier when they provide a higher level of empathy and understanding towards their customers. Especially those who are being the most difficult with them at any given time. In fact, the hallmark of an outstanding customer service provider is someone who can provide extra attention to the people who are the most upset, angry, and demanding, and sometimes even the ones who are being the most abusive.

I am not saying that Awesome Adjusters never get frustrated. I'm not saying that they don't feel annoyed, angry, irritated, or even exasperated. Those feelings are perfectly normal in our business, and we have to accept them. What I am suggesting is that Awesome Adjusters omit the name calling. They tell their coworkers that they are frustrated with what happened, maybe let one of their co-workers know that they are exhausted from talking to an extremely demanding person.

Just drop the idiot, the jerk, and the moron comments, and it will automatically alter your approach to your customers. Awesome claims adjusters recognize that their job is to help people. That means dealing with people who can be upset and angry and annoyed. The awesome claims adjuster is one whose attitude is, "Yes, this person's being really difficult right now, but they are the ones who've been involved in the accident, not me. So the way I can help is to take a little bit more time and be a little bit more patient, and not take on the anger myself."

During the middle of one of my training classes on customer service, an adjuster came up to me one time and said, "Carl, you are always harping on about the customers. You are always saying the customer is so important. Don't you know you are talking about the enemy?"

This adjuster referred to dealing with his customers as "dealing with the enemy." When he said that to me, I couldn't help but feel sorry for him. How horrible it must be to come to work every day thinking you're facing "the enemy." I could see it in his eyes. He saw the people he had to deal with, the insureds, the claimants and everyone else, as the enemy that brings him down. They attack him, they lie to him, they challenge him, and every day he has to fight for his survival. He saw it that way.

Is there any chance at all, that because his attitude towards his customers is that they are "the enemy" that he treats them that way? Is there any possibility that because he sees them as the enemy, that he is consistent with the things that he says or how he explains things to them. When he is faced with someone who doesn't understand, is it possible that since that person is "the enemy" that he's not very patient, and maybe even demanding, and sometimes attacks when he thinks he's being attacked? My guess is, and it's only a guess, that this poor adjuster treats people in a way that is very consistent with how he perceives them. He perceives them as the enemy, and that's going to come out in his behavior.

Even though we think it doesn't come out (because we hang up before we call people idiots, jerks, and morons), there is absolutely no way to mask this attitude when it comes to dealing with customers. We think we can mask it, which is why of course we think it's okay. I'll agree that to call someone an idiot, a jerk, or a moron, after you hang up is not as bad as thinking that they are the enemy. But there is no way to believe that customers are idiots, jerks, and morons, and not have it affect the way we treat them. It is absolutely impossible to always mask how we feel all the time, and it will come out.

Now that I've said this, let me state a qualifier. None of this is the claims adjuster's fault. Absolutely none. The fact that adjusters can run around calling customers idiots, jerks, and morons, is not the fault of the claims adjusters.

This is absolutely, positively, management's fault. This is a management failure. The reason this is a management failure is very simple; because management lets it happen. In fact, sometimes management even joins in on the laughter and the name-calling. I know because I was a claim manager, and I let it happen. The whole idea that a management team can train empathy into claims people while they themselves are allowing this negativism to persist is laughable. This is management's failure, not the failure of the claims adjuster.

I preach this issue strongly in my customer service classes and I am not afraid to let the managers in the group know that this is entirely their fault. Most of them believe me, while many still want to hold onto their belief that this is all harmless. But I was very pleased one day when I happened to come into a claims office a couple days after one of my customer service classes to hear something. I overheard an adjuster, who had not been to the class yet, go to his manager, who had been to the class, and say, "Oh man, you wouldn't believe this idiot!" The manager, much to my pleasure, responded by saying, "Well look, I don't know if he's an idiot, but he obviously needs some help, let's see what we can do for him. What's the problem?"

It won't take very long in that office, maybe a week or two, before people stop running around calling customers idiots, jerks, and morons, if the manager stops. People tend to emulate their managers, and as long as the manager feels it's okay, believe me, it's going to be okay in that office.

As you are reading this book, you are now responsible for changing yourself. If you are a claims adjuster, you can't wait for management to correct its failure, you can correct it yourself. Awesome claims adjusters don't wait for management to solve their problems. Awesome claims adjusters recognize that improvement is needed in themselves and they do not wait around for other people to point it out to them. They don't hide in management's sometimes shortsightedness. They go forward and do the right thing.

In this case, if you are thinking that it's okay to keep name calling because your supervisor or manager does, then you haven't quite got the idea of becoming an awesome claims adjuster. If, however, you realize that although it goes on in your office, you yourself have the opportunity to make a change because you can change the attitude towards your customer, you are on the path toward being a great adjuster.

CHAPTER 8

Desire for Excellence

Of all the characteristics you will find in this book, this is the most easily attained, and the most often ignored characteristic for claims adjusters. Please do not confuse the desire for excellence with being a perfectionist. I know many perfectionists, and some make terrible adjusters. People who simply cannot live unless everything is absolutely perfect, can get easily frustrated in the claims world. Awesome Adjusters don't want everything perfect, but they do have the desire to do an outstanding job. Doing a great job is more pleasing to them than doing a mediocre job.

A perfectionist usually drives everyone around them nuts because they want things absolutely perfect. However, an adjuster that does what he's asked to do, and always does an excellent job in what he is asked to do, is usually much more productive and valuable in the claims arena.

To be productive and valuable, one must see one's responsibilities, whatever they are, as important, and worth doing well. To illustrate my point, I would like to tell you about one of the most important days in my entire career. More than 20 years later, I refer to it only as That Day.

THAT DAY

When I was hired by my first insurance company, I was not immediately put into a claims position. I suppose they wanted to test me out to see whether or not I could do as I was told, so I was placed in the file room. I was asked to help make photocopies for the adjusters. Now keep in mind, back when I first started in the insurance business in 1980, photocopy machines were simple but time-consuming. Our claims operation had a person who was responsible for making all of the photocopies for the department, and that is what this person did all the time. Well, this was me for a while.

Actually, there were three of us in the file room that would make photocopies for all of the adjusters. That's all we did, and we worked in shifts. When I first reported to do the photocopies, I met the other two individuals who were going to be doing the copying as well. I thought surely there was a mistake, for someone as intelligent as myself couldn't possibly be working with these two people!

The first guy I just know was mentally challenged. The other guy could barely read English and had this weird lopsided smile made you want to turn your head a bit when you were talking to him. These were not very bright guys, and I would have been surprised to hear that they even graduated the sixth grade. And here we were working side by side. And here I was, a high school graduate . . . imagine that!

After a few days, I decided I had had enough, and I went to my supervisor, and told him I desired to be promoted into the unit that takes loss reports. He noted my desire and asked me to go back to do my work. Knowing that my future included much bigger things than making photocopies, I didn't take my work too seriously. After all, this was just photocopying. Any idiot could do it. As a matter of fact, there were a couple of idiots doing it right then. I deserved better, and I deserved to be out of this place, I told myself.

When adjusters would come to me with their files to be photocopied, and wanted to know when it would be done, I would roll my eyes and say "It will be done when it's done, what's the big deal?" The other two guys (those dummies) would get all bent out of shape and go into a panic if they cut off something from the photocopy that they were making. If something was a little bit twisted on the page, they would stand there and figure out how to bend the paper just right to make sure every single piece was photocopied. It seemed ridiculous to me. This was just photocopying, for crying out loud.

When adjusters would approach these Bozos and ask when their files would be done, these dopes would give them an exact time and swear that it would be done by then. Sure enough, they worked like maniacs to get it done on time. When adjusters would come to me and ask when their files would be done, my response would be, "Don't worry, it will get done. At some point before this machine breaks down, I will get it done." I was cool and deserved better.

Needless to say, it was hard to take this work seriously. Like I said, I was meant for bigger and better things. I will have to admit that it was fun to watch these two guys run around taking their job so seriously and making sure everything was right. It made me feel sorry for them. They had such little minds and such little imaginations, that this was probably the most important thing that they were ever going to be asked to do in their lives, and they acted that way.

I would have been embarrassed to act that way. In fact, even asking the adjusters questions on what they wanted and how they wanted it seemed like an embarrassing routine for me to even engage in, so most of the time I wouldn't even ask. "If the adjusters didn't like what I did," I would think to myself, "then they could give it to one of the two nerds to get it done." That's how I felt.

After what seemed to be an eternity (about four weeks), I went to my supervisor, and made the following plea, "I can't take it in there anymore. This is just photocopying, and it is really mindless. It takes no intelligence to do my job. It takes no skill, no initiative, and no integrity. It is the most basic and simple job there is!"

As I was saying this, I decided that I would be gracious and accept my supervisor's apology which was sure to come swiftly. I would accept an abrupt move to the Loss Report unit. Perhaps he might take me to lunch to further extend his apology for leaving such a skilled and talented individual wallowing in unnecessary and menial work for so long. Who knows? I suppose a raise wouldn't have been out of line, but I didn't want to be too greedy.

My supervisor had a slightly different response than the one I was expecting. He looked up at me and he said, "Carl, you're right. That job does not take any skill. It takes no intelligence whatsoever. It takes no initiative, and really almost any idiot can do that job . . . and you are not even the best one!"

Those proverbial bricks hit hard when they landed on me. What was going on here? You mean I am going to be judged on the work that I do, and not how brilliant I am? You mean I am going to be judged on results? How unfair!

It's funny, but it never dawned on me that people saw me by the work that I did. I judged myself by what I was capable of, but others were judging me by what I did. I am very, very fortunate that I learned this lesson back when I first started in this industry. It almost didn't happen. I could have easily obtained that Loss Report taking job, and quickly thought that was beneath me.

I could have received my first adjusting job and thought that was beneath me. I could have continued in my career, always thinking that I was meant for better things, and never taking things seriously, and never looking at my current job as the indispensable part of what I needed to be successful in order to move on.

I have known many people like this. People who look at their job of being a claims adjuster as not the most important thing in the world. I have seen people go through their whole careers without understanding how crucial it is to want to do an outstanding job because people see you for what you do. I am very often asked by claims adjusters in the classes that I teach, on how to become claims managers, district managers, even claims vice presidents. My response is very simple. Whatever job that you have now, is the most important job that you will ever have, because it is an indispensable step that will move you to your next job. Treat it that way.

You say you want an example? Okay, here you go then. I would like to introduce you to someone who excelled in the characteristic of desiring to do an excellent job. I met him a year or so after That Day. His name was Scott, and this guy was no jerk.

SCOTT THE NO-JERK

As a young claims adjuster with a year's worth of experience in auto property damage, I was asked to help out in the subrogation department for a period of time; just a few months. After about two months, I found that it was pretty easy to excel in this subrogation unit because, for whatever reason, the company that I was working for at the time did not put their best people in the subrogation department. It was more of a dumping ground.

In fact, after about two months, I was the top money collector in the unit. While the other subrogation adjusters were sending out their 8th, 9th and 10th subrogation notice after receiving no response on the first seven, I was making a phone call after my 1st. If I couldn't get what I wanted after one letter, I would file arbitration. For some reason, the other subro adjusters just didn't like filing arbitration, but I saw it as a quick way to get the issue resolved. Win or lose, at least it was going to be over with.

One day while talking to my supervisor, complaining that I needed someone else in the unit that wasn't a complete jerk to help pull the weight, I was told that I didn't need to worry about it anymore; they had just hired a new trainee, someone brand new in the insurance business that I could train to take my spot.

I was elated. "Oh thank God," I said, "Please tell me you didn't hire some jerk. If we get one more jerk in this unit, we are going to have to change our name from the Subrogation unit to the Jerkogation unit. What's his name?" My supervisor responded with, "Scott Jerk."

"JERK! The guy's name is JERK!?" I reeled. "You finally hire someone else to help me, and you hire a guy already named Jerk, what good is that?"

It turns out his name was not J E R K, but Jurek. Scott Jurek knew absolutely nothing about insurance; as a matter of fact he spent most of his time at lunch and break talking about music. I think he wanted to be a band leader in real life, but he certainly seemed to have a good head on his shoulders. I noticed that Scott was a quick learner and never seemed to mind when asked to do certain things, even when I couldn't explain why we were doing them.

As the new top dog in the subrogation department, I was asked to proof read everyone else's arbitration forms before giving them to our supervisor to check (we did a lot of double-checking at this company). The routine went like this. I would give a stack to my supervisor, and stand there while he briefly checked them. He would ask, "Carl, did June double check her work to be certain she filled out all of her paperwork correctly?" I would reply, "Well, she said she did." My supervisor would then check through the forms, pass on the ones that looked right, and hand me back the ones that weren't completed properly.

What's important to know is that to complete these forms did not take a lot of brains. It did not even take much skill. It simply took paying attention and being careful. Anyone in the subrogation department could fill out these forms completely with no errors if they were simply paying attention. That's why our supervisor would always ask if we double-checked them. And most of us would say yes, even if we didn't.

My supervisor would then ask, "Carl, did Linda double check her work to be sure she completed the subrogation forms properly?" My response again would be, "Well, she said she did." My supervisor would then review them and again pass on anything that looked correct and hand me back anything that might have had errors.

When it came to my pile, he would ask, "Carl, did you double-check to make sure you filled out everything correctly?" And I would say, "Yes." He would check them as he did with everybody else, and although I had a much higher rate of the form being completed correctly, every once in a while, he would find one with errors. On those occasions, he would hand it back to me and say, "Are you sure you double checked them?" knowing full well I hadn't, or else I would have caught the error.

This sounds a little mundane, but I should tell you that one day something extraordinary happened. I gave the stack of arbitration forms to my supervisor, and he went through asking me again one-by-one if everybody completed the forms. When he got to Scott's, he asked me, "Carl, did Scott double check his work?" My response was "He said he did." My supervisor did something at that point that absolutely amazed me. More than amazed me, I was absolutely floored. My supervisor invoked what I now call The Scott Reality.

THE SCOTT REALITY

After asking me if Scott had double-checked his work, and hearing my usual reply of "he said he did," my supervisor took the stack of Scott's arbitration forms and simply put them in the pile as "approved" and did not even bother to look at them. This took me quite by surprise, and being a little puzzled, I asked my supervisor, "Why is it that you are checking all of the other adjuster's arbitration forms, and even my arbitration forms, and you are not checking Scott's?"

My supervisor looked up at me, and said, "Carl, if Scott says he double-checked them, then that means he did double-check them."

Like I said, I was absolutely floored. What was going on here? How was it that Scott, after just a few weeks in the department was already doing work at a quality level so high that my supervisor decided he didn't even need to bother to check?

I spent the next few weeks keeping an eye on this Jurek character, trying to figure out what his game was. Sure enough, I found his little trick. You see, when Scott said he did something, he really did it. The reality of the situation was, if the supervisor said to use black ink instead of blue, he used black ink. If he was asked to proofread all the letters before they were sent out, he proofread them. If Scott was asked to make a second copy of contentions and staple them upside down in the file folder, then that's what he did.

The reality was, Scott liked doing a good job. As a matter of fact, he liked

144

doing an excellent job. I will admit that through the years I certainly took my share of short-cuts. I have never met an adjuster who said he had too much time during the day and he was bored. Every adjuster I have met in my entire career says they do not have enough time to get everything done. So cutting corners is just part of the natural evolution I suppose, but it certainly didn't seem that way for Scott.

In spending time with Scott over the next few months, I found out something very interesting. Not only did he enjoy doing an excellent job, he liked the fact that people could trust him when he said he was going to get something done.

The desire to do an outstanding job is possible to develop. Most of the time, the desire to do an excellent job comes from personal values instilled at an early age, but it sometimes can be learned. To learn the desire for excellence, one must be exposed to the rewards. This is management's greatest failing: the practice of attempting to train employees to desire excellence without showing potential rewards. How does anyone know that they want something until they have tried it or seen it?

Scott already had the desire for excellence when he became an adjuster. He knew that meant that even the little boring things have to get done, like making sure the form is complete, getting a statement when one is needed, documenting the file, attaching the photos in the right place, using the right color ink. Why? Because Scott knew that no one could see his good hard work if their attention has been distracted by the little things.

A crucial issue here is that the desire for excellence does not impede the ability to accept feedback and constructive criticism. Pride in one's work is an essential element in the desire for excellence; however, it cannot stand in the way of accepting that improvement is possible and should be sought.

I don't have to tell you that in a very short period of time, Scott's recoveries far exceeded mine. While I was wasting time redoing work, because I wasn't thorough enough to want to do an excellent job in the first place, Scott was moving on to other files.

Scott Jurek is now a claims executive for a regional insurance company. He has been put in charge of claims operations in several states and serves on the Claims Leadership Team. But once upon a time, he was a subrogation adjuster trainee in a small office in Los Angeles, at a desk next to mine. And I was fortunate to have been a friend of his, because it taught me a lesson that would benefit me through the rest of my career. The Scott Reality was going to hit home and hit hard.

THE SCOTT REALITY (AS PERFORMED BY CARL)

After watching Scott become successful, I decided that I wanted to have what he had. I wanted to have my supervisor and management team so confident in me that they didn't even have to check my work. I realized that it didn't matter what I thought of myself, that people saw me for the work that I did. I guess that it is true that "we tend to judge ourselves by what we think we are capable of, but others judge us by what we do."

It is funny — and tragic at the same time — but I have met so many talented individuals that work 15, 20, 30 years in their careers, and it never dawns on them that they should be outstanding at what they do. It never hits them that the work they do is who they are. They kind of just continue on through their lives, being content with being average. Well, I decided that wasn't for me, so I was going to put The Scott Reality (the desire for excellence) to my benefit.

After leaving the subrogation department, and passing through the Bodily Injury Unit, I ended up as an Auto Field Adjuster. I wanted this badly, mostly because I wanted the company car. Nevertheless, I saw this as an opportunity to learn something new, having been through the other departments.

One of my first assignments was to write automobile estimates on Total Loss cars in a Field Inspection Station. To practice my estimating skills, I was told to write estimates on the total losses that got towed into the tow yard. I was housed in a smoky, partially air-conditioned trailer on the back lot of a tow yard with five other appraisers. Each day our supervisor would hand out assignments for the day, and we would run out feverishly to write the estimates to justify the total loss of the cars. (Okay, you got me. We wandered out begrudgingly after 25 minutes of complaining).

Writing estimates on these cars wasn't difficult, most of the time, because the cars were totally wrecked. Nevertheless, we were told to write an estimate on every single car no matter how badly damaged. This seemed absurd of course, because sometimes when they were so completely burned, you couldn't distinguish a single piece on the car. But that was the rule.

Just to be silly, when a car was brought in that was completely demolished, my good friend Ken Sanders would write on his estimate, "Lift up radiator cap. Replace car. Lower radiator cap. $30,000."

Ken got promoted and left me there with the others. One of the things we were asked to do, even though it seemed silly to us, was to always do an inventory of the equipment on each vehicle. This doesn't seem like much of a burden, but to us it seemed very burdensome. Especially when sometimes out on the tow yard, the temperature reached 120 degrees in the burning sun, and sometimes much hotter than that inside the car we were supposed to check.

Other times, it could be pouring rain all day, and we still had to go out there and crawl around in the mud to check every single piece of equipment on the car, such as cruise control, sunroof, power seats, etc. I didn't realize it then, but I found out later that this was important because the percentage of salvage we were paid was based on a percentage of the actual cash value in the total loss settlement. That, of course, was determined by what kind of equipment the car had on it. But I didn't know it then, so to me it just seemed silly.

On particularly nasty days, instead of actually going out and writing down what type of optional equipment they had, the easy way out was to call the insured and ask them what equipment the car had. The vast majority of the insured would tell the truth because they figured you would find out if it was a lie anyway. An adjuster could simply note those items and turn in the paperwork. A short cut, yes, but a reasonable one.

The very first time it was pouring rain outside, I started to head out to look at a car, and I was asked by a coworker why I was going out into the rain. When I told him I had to check all of the optional equipment on the car, I was given the option by him in the following manner: "You dummy. Just call the insured and get the equipment from the insured. Why do you go out slop-ping in the rain like a jerk? The car is a total loss anyway, so what's the big deal?"

Had he not used the work jerk, I may not have made the connection. But he did, and I remembered The Scott Reality. I had a desire for excellence, and that meant doing what I was supposed to do.

I didn't have a good answer for him, other than it was what I was asked to do, but I certainly couldn't say that. So I didn't answer at all, and just kept doing what I was supposed to do.

After a few months, it was pretty clear that Ken and I were the only ones out of the six of us actually going out every single time. All of the other adjusters would use the easy method and call the insured. The real sloppy guys called the insured almost every time. The average adjusters actually looked at the car most of the time. One really good guy I worked with looked at the cars almost all of the time and would only call the insured when it was extreme-ly bad weather. Ken and I on the other hand, went out and checked every single time. Why? Because Scott had taught me a lesson, and I didn't want to lose sight of it.

I will admit, however, that I was starting to feel foolish. Months and months had gone by, and I was the only one going out and checking every piece of equipment. I actually did start to feel like a twit and thought that maybe this total commitment was not worth it. Until one day, I watched a confrontation between my manager and the owner of the tow yard.

They were standing inside the trailer, arguing about the value of the cars and what was owed to our company by the tow yard. This happened quite a bit, as the tow yard seemed to find a way to argue about every little thing. I never paid much attention, until it centered on me.

The tow yard owner was trying to show our manager our sloppy work. He was complaining that our sloppy work was costing him money, because he was paying more for the salvage that he should, because we were paying more for the total losses than we should. He had a stack in his hand and wanted to go over them. I was surprised that this was being done right in front of us, and nobody could get any work done as we watched the drama unfold.

Wouldn't you know it, but the very first one was mine! It was a total loss I had written on a 1974 Toyota pickup. The tow yard manager yelled, "Look at this one that Van did! It's a '74 Toyota pickup, and he's got that it has cruise control on it! What kind of bullshit is this?"

I will never forget what happened next. My manager grabbed the file, looked at it for a moment, looked at me, looked back at the tow yard manager, and said, "If Van says there is cruise control on that car, then there is cruise control on that car." And he threw the file down on the desk and walked out of the trailer and into the coffee shop next door. The other adjusters looked at me, and I sank in my chair. I got a lump in my throat and a very heavy feeling in my stomach. I blew it.

I thought to myself that there was no way a 1974 Toyota pickup truck has cruise control on it. That's ridiculous. I couldn't believe this; after all of the running out in bad weather trying to do the right thing, I am going to get nailed for a simple mistake I made. I must have been looking at the wrong car. What other explanation could there be? Six months of slopping through that muck trying to do the right thing is now going to blow up in my face. Every time one of my co-workers told me I was wasting my time, I shrugged them off. Now I was concerned that they might have been right.

After my manager walked out, the tow yard owner started chasing after him. Needless to say, I put my head on my desk, clasped my hands together, and began to pray, "Please God, let there be cruise control on that pickup . . . Please God, let there be cruise control on that pickup . . . Please God, let there be cruise control on that pickup."

One of my coworkers grabbed the file and dashed out of the trailer. The other five followed immediately. Reluctantly, I had to find out myself, so I was the last out of the trailer. As I came upon the '74 pickup in question, I saw the other adjusters looking in the car and shaking their heads. The last guy to look in the car looked at the steering wheel where the cruise control button would be, looked over at me, rolled his eyes, shook his head, and walked away.

As I walked up to the car I started to remember writing it up . . . no 1974 Toyota pickup truck comes with cruise control, even as an option, so there was no way it could have had it, but I still had to check anyway.

I ducked my head in the car, and looked at the turn indicator. Sure enough, I saw the words, "Resume; Accel; Set." Those are the unmistakable words that in fact meant cruise control was installed on this car. Apparently, the owner of the car was a mechanic, and he installed it himself. We don't even know how he got it to work, and maybe it didn't even work, that really wasn't the point. The point was that there was a cruise control mechanism in the car and I had it written down (Thank You, Lord!).

My manager had a level of faith in me that I could never have achieved by taking shortcuts. I could never have gained his level of confidence by doing things right only most of the time. It took an absolute dedication to doing an outstanding job, 100% of the time.

Is the desire for excellence an easy skill to develop? Well, of all the characteristics, it's the one most in each person's control. All that it takes is the decision that you want something. You want to be viewed as someone who does an outstanding job in everything that you do. And as I mentioned before, that doesn't mean being perfect, it simply means having the attitude that you might as well do an outstanding job of it, as opposed to cutting corners and hoping for the best. Awesome Adjusters have the desire for excellence.

CHAPTER 9

Teamwork

The most important aspect in the area of teamwork is for claims people to understand what teamwork really is. Because claims people have the opportunity to work by themselves, on their own cases and files, and only interact on a limited basis, we believe that teamwork is not important in claims. In fact, we believe that we can do an outstanding job with our own files and work, while someone right next to us struggles, falters, and fails. We believe this for a very important reason: it's true.

We really can do a very good job in claims on our own files, while other people struggle; however, that doesn't mean we can't improve teamwork as well. One characteristic of Awesome Adjusters is not only that they do a great job on their own work, but they also help out in the office. They understand that by helping other people they will get the rewards themselves later on, and that will make all of their jobs much easier. I'd like to take you through some examples to see how if we all helped each other, it would reduce the work we all have.

WHAT BUSINESS ARE YOU IN?

When I monitor phone calls, one of the most important questions I have to answer for myself is:

Is this adjuster in the "customer service" business?

or,

Is this adjuster in the "get rid of this person if he's not my problem" business?

That's right, the most important thing I listen for is to see whether or not a claims adjuster actually believes his job is customer service and is willing to help even if it's not his claim, or does the adjuster try to do anything he can to get rid of a customer because it's not his problem? The reason this is important in the area of teamwork is because there's a huge potential that we're all creating more work for ourselves by being selfish and only handling our own work. Here's my example:

I'm listening to phone calls one day when a particular call came in that I believe makes my point. A customer, Betsy Burke, called and got Maria, and the exchange went like this:

Maria: *Hello, this is Maria in claims, how can I help you?*

Betsy: *Yes, I'm calling in to find out what's going on. I keep getting calls from the company that loaned me money on the car. I thought you guys paid this off, what's going on?*

Maria: *Oh, this is Tom's claim, he's not in today, can I have him call you tomorrow?*

Betsy: *No, I want to find out what's going on now.*

Maria: (a big sigh) *Okay, what is your claim number?*

Betsy: *1234567*

Maria: *Okay, it looks here like we paid $6000 on your truck.*

Betsy: *But I owe $8,000.*

Maria: *Hold on* (Maria puts Betsy on hold, two minutes pass)

Maria: (gets back on the phone) *Ma'am, did you sign a bill of sale?*

Betsy: *A bill of sale? What's that?*

Marie: (Click. Put on hold again, doesn't say a word before doing
                this)

(Three minutes pass. The phone rings and a new person answers the phone)

Steve: *Hello, this is Steve, claims supervisor, can I help you?*

Now let's take a look at this exchange. Let me ask you, reading this exchange
right now, do you believe Maria is in the "customer service" business, or is
she in the "get rid of this lady, she's not my problem" business? That's right,
this adjuster is in the "get rid of this lady, she's not my problem" business.
Notice how she didn't even want to try to help. Her first goal was to try to
get rid of this woman.

Now, in the adjuster's defense, you might say that maybe she wasn't supposed
to answer these questions or maybe she didn't know how to help someone
like this. That would be a good defense except she knew perfectly how to do
it. That's not why she wasn't helping this person. She wasn't helping this
person, because it wasn't her claim and therefore it wasn't her job. You see,
she doesn't know she's in the customer service business, she thinks she's in
the handling claims business.

Take a look at the next phase, when she realized that she was going to have
to talk to this person a big sigh came out, which is clearly telling the customer that she really doesn't want to deal with it but she's willing to put up
with it. This isn't great customer service and these types of things come out
more than we can ever imagine.

When she put the customer on hold the first time, she did say "hold on." But
what's just common courtesy when you put someone on hold? It's common
courtesy to simply ask someone if they can be put on hold. Such as, "Would
you mind if I put you on hold?" And of course, it's always nice to actually
wait for an answer. Additionally, it's common courtesy to tell someone how

long they're going to be put on hold, and maybe even give them a reason for being put on hold. Unfortunately, we didn't get any of that; what we got was, "hold on."

You might be looking at this conversation wondering how this claims supervisor got involved in this. For that, I need to reconstruct the telephone call because it's not obvious from just listening to this. I had to go out to the office where this was taking place and reconstruct it. Basically, what happened was the first time Maria put the customer on hold she walked over to her supervisor and said,

Maria: *Hey, Steve, this is Tom's claim, he's not here right now. Can I transfer this call to you?*

Steve: *What does she want?*

Maria: *I don't know, something about we paid $6,000 but she owes $8,000. Can I transfer this call to you?*

Steve: *Well, she must have signed a Bill of Sale or something, didn't she?*

Maria: *I'll go find out.*

Now this is the point where Maria gets back on the phone and asks the person if she signed a bill of sale. When the customer shows that she doesn't even know what a bill of sale is, Maria puts her right back on hold and this time doesn't even bother saying "hold on." She just puts Betsy on hold. Then Maria walks back over to her supervisor.

Maria: *She doesn't even know what a Bill of Sale is. Can I transfer this call to you?*

Steve: *Fine, fine, transfer the call to me.*

Maria walks back to her desk, clicks on the line, transfers the call, and hangs

155

up the phone. And that ends her total interaction with this customer. So let me ask, do you think she is saving herself any time? Do you think she is saving herself any work? Well there's one thing for sure Maria thinks she has done. She thinks she has saved herself work by not having to deal with this person at all and trying to get rid of this call. Yet, if everybody in the office is doing the same thing, it's actually generating more work for everyone.

The idea behind teamwork is that if everyone, before they try to get rid of a customer, can at least see if they can help the customer, it will actually reduce the work that all of us have. Because, if Maria had gotten rid of this call by taking a message for Tom, then all that means is that Tom has to call back the next day. And when he does call back and doesn't get the person, he'll leave a voice mail message. And when that person calls back she won't get Tom, because Tom will be on the phone, and then he'll leave a voice mail message. And then Tom will call back the customer and maybe after about five or six phone calls back and forth, Tom might actually be able to talk to this person and do absolutely nothing more for this person than anyone else could have done.

What I want to submit is that if everyone simply tried to help customers, if they could, before they try to get rid of the person, it would reduce the amount of work for everybody. This is where the teamwork aspect comes in.

I've talked to plenty of adjusters who thought they were outstanding in teamwork. In fact, I asked one adjuster one day if he thought he was good at teamwork and he said, yes, he thought he was outstanding. When I asked him why, he replied, "Simple, I am great at teamwork because I do my job, and pull my own weight, and I don't bug anybody else."

Believe it or not, this adjuster thought he was outstanding at teamwork because he never asked anybody else to do anything for him, he always did his own work and never bothered anybody. To him, this is teamwork.

Teamwork is a much higher level then just doing your own work and minding your own business.

Awesome claims adjusters understand that they will get back far more than they will ever give by paying attention to teamwork. Helping others in their office will always give them great rewards, because they will almost always get paid back more than they ever offered in the first place. Additionally, Awesome Adjusters know that helping customers whenever they can, even if it's not their file, will ultimately reduce the amount of work the entire office has, and everyone benefits.

CHAPTER 10

Initiative

Imagine you are a claims supervisor. Two of your adjusters, Stann Rose and Dopey McClaim, come up to you on the same day with essentially the same situation. Which one would you want working for you?

Dopey: *Is Med Pay subrogateable in California?*

You: *In some situations.*

Dopey: *What situations?*

You: *Alright, let's go over it . . .* Blah, blah, blah.

After taking 30 minutes to go over all that, Dopey leaves. A little while later Stann comes up to you and says:

Stann: *I have a question.*

You: *What is it?*

Stann: *Well, I have a claim where I need to figure out if Med Pay is Subrogateable in California. So first, I asked a couple of senior adjusters in the office, and they gave me some info but not enough to conclude whether it applies in this case. So then I went to the FC&S books and found a case similar to mine. It helped me, but still I couldn't nail it down. So then I called our in-house counsel, and they gave me the name of a law firm they use in California*

158

> sometimes, Dew, Knot, Winn & Pay. I called them and Mr. Winn
> told me about a case in California about Subrogateable rights for
> Med Pay in California, but advised me it really came down to the
> wording of the policy.

You: *Yeah . . .*

Stann: *So I looked up the case he referred to and found out what policy was*
analyzed in the court case. I got a copy of that policy and read it. It
appears that the wording of that policy and our policy is very simi-
lar, with just a slight variation. After looking at it for a while, I
believe that the case would apply, and that we are entitled to subro
for our damages, but I would like to go over it with you.

So, again, you are the claims supervisor. Which adjuster would you rather have working for you?

My guess is that you would rather have Stann working for you. Why? Because Stann demonstrated a high level of initiative. Is Dopey a bad claims adjuster? Of course not. In fact, he is average. Most of us operate just as Dopey did. When we have a question, we ask our supervisor. Stann, however, took steps that showed initiative.

Because of that, Stann will gain knowledge in his career five times faster than Dopey can ever hope to. Because, you see, along the way, while researching his answer, Stann gained a great deal of knowledge in many other areas that Dopey will never even be exposed to.

Just so you know, Stann is a top claims executive for a national insurer. But once upon a time, he was an adjuster and I was his supervisor. Stann constantly demonstrated a high level of initiative from day one. I didn't instill it in him. He just had it when I met him. Nevertheless, I've seen that characteristic in every awesome claims adjuster I've ever met.

That's true of Tom Del Corso. He is a regional claims manager now, but once was an adjuster of mine. And Tom, like Stann, had a high level of initiative that helped him learn and grow faster than everyone else around him.

By the time Tom came to me with a question, I was confident he had done his homework and had thought things through. Even if he was wrong in his conclusion, it was the effort he made and the initiative he displayed that I most appreciated.

A good adjuster: one who comes to his supervisor for answers because he is concerned with doing things right.

An excellent adjuster: one who follows his supervisor's suggestions on where to go to find the answers.

An Awesome Adjuster: one who feels obligated to do as much legwork and analysis as he can on his own and then comes to his supervisor for guidance.

Please pay careful attention to the fact that I used the words "feels obligated." Those words will be key if you would like to learn a simple initiative-building technique.

Can initiative be learned? Well, it's not easy, but it's not impossible. But it is VERY important to describe what we mean by initiative. Most adjusters don't really appreciate it. Even most supervisors do not fully appreciate what initiative really is and therefore have no way of instilling it in their adjusters.

We teach a full-day class on just Attitude and Initiative Training for Claims Adjusters. Believe me, it is not a quick thing. Therefore, I cannot outline everything you would need to know to instill a high level of initiative in yourself or in someone else. I can, however, give you one simple little training technique that, if you apply it, will absolutely increase the amount of initiative you display 300% in just a month or so.

Interested? If so, you'll have to put up with a little challenge that I give to my

Teaching and Coaching for Claims Supervisors and Managers students. The point of the challenge is to get people to think of what initiative really is. In that class, I ask the following question, "How do you instill initiative in your adjusters?

Here is how the conversation goes:

Carl: *So, is initiative important? Would you rather have Stann working for you or Dopey?*

1st student: *Yes, initiative is extremely important. I'd rather have Stann working for me.*

Carl: *So how do you instill initiative in your adjusters?*

2nd Student: *I always tell them to read their policy before they come to me.*

Carl: *Then that's not initiative. They are just doing what you told them to. Initiative is doing it on their own before they are told. In your case, they are just carrying out your orders.*

3rd student: *I always tell them to research something and come to me with a suggestion on what they think the answer is.*

Carl: *Again, that's not initiative. You told them to do it. They are just following your directions. Don't get me wrong, if they carry out your orders by checking something out before coming to you, that is better than if they just come to you directly, but it's still not initiative. You had to tell them to do it.*

4th student: *I tell them they need to take the initiative to find the answer on their own.*

Carl: *That's not initiative. They are just following your orders. Remember, initiative is where they take steps on their own without your telling*

161

them to do it. They do it out of a sense of obligation. How do you instill initiative in your adjusters without telling them what to do?

At this point in the class, I usually get some puzzled looks. My students begin to realize the Catch 22 here. You can't tell someone to take initiative, and have it truly be initiative.

Carl: Does anyone, right now, have someone working for you like Stann and Tom?

Class: We wish.

Carl: So whatever you are doing now to instill initiative in your people is not working. What's the proof? The proof is you don't have anybody like Stann and Tom. You said you would like someone like that. So, all you have to do is do a little training.

At this stage, my students want to know the answer. But, as I mentioned, I can't deliver a whole class worth of training in one chapter, but I can give a quick example of what we train supervisors to do and suggest a way for anyone to incorporate it into their own behavior. One simple question should do it. The golden question.

THE GOLDEN QUESTION

In our Teaching and Coaching for Claims Supervisors and Managers class I referenced above, I usually pose a question. I am going to present this in the conversation format because I want you, the reader, to draw the conclusions my students would. To instill initiative, you must train people differently than you would train them in most other concepts. To do this, I pose a question to the class and go around the room to see if I can find the right answer.

Carl: An adjuster, call her Rebecca Hughes, comes up to you and asks if Med Pay is subrogatable in California. What to you tell her?

1st Student: *I tell her to research it for herself.*

Carl: *No, that is giving orders, and as we discussed, you can't order someone to create initiative. They have to think of it on their own.*

2nd Student: *I'd ask her what she thinks.*

Carl: *That won't help, because she doesn't know, and she'll tell you so.*

3rd Student: *I'd tell her she has to take initiative, and to figure it out for herself.*

Carl: *No good. If you tell someone to take initiative, and they follow your orders, that's not initiative.*

4th Student: *I'd tell her not to bug me until after lunch.*

Carl: *At least that will work for a while.*

5th Student: *I'd . . . I'd . . . I don't know what I'd do anymore.*

Carl: *Ah, you see how hard it is to think of a way to get someone to do something without telling them? That is the challenge. We have to get Rebecca to feel obligated to go off and do a little research on her own, WITHOUT telling her to.*

   To do that, you are going to ask The Golden Question. It is the question that you will ask over and over again. When Rebecca comes to you and asks her question, your response is always:

What steps did you take to get the answer before coming to me?

So, let's watch how this works. Rebecca comes up to you and asks if Med Pay is subrogateable in California, and you ask, "What steps did you take to get the answer before coming to me?" Rebecca will have done nothing of course, and she says, "Nothing."

Do you give her the answer?

Class: *NO!!*

Carl: *Does everyone agree you should not give Rebecca the answer?*

Class: *Yes.*

Carl: *Sorry, that's wrong. You absolutely give her the answer.*

Class: *No way!!*

Carl: *Yes, you give her the answer. Assuming you know it. You give her the answer immediately after she just admitted she did nothing to deserve the answer. Then let her leave and forget it.*

Now, the next time she comes to you with a question, you do exactly the same thing. You ask, "What steps did you take to get the answer before coming to me?" She might say she did nothing again, and again you give her the answer and let her leave. Without your telling her, you've let her know she didn't quite meet your expectations. She feels a slight pang, but she's too busy right now to worry about it, so she goes back to her work.

It may take three, four, maybe five times, but pretty soon Rebecca is going to be expecting that question. She knows she's been getting those answers for free, and has not lived up to your expectation. After a while, she is going to feel obligated to have done something before coming to you. And that feeling of obligation is the exact thing you are looking to create.

6th Student: *I don't see how.*

Carl: *Imagine you go to lunch with a friend. As lunch is ending, you say, "Let me get the check this time," and you pay for lunch. The next* time you go to lunch with your friend, what would you expect? Wouldn't you expect that he would pay for lunch? More importantly, wouldn't he expect to pay for lunch?

6th Student: Not MY friends.

Carl: Well, most normal people then. Wouldn't they expect to pay for lunch next time?

6th Student: Yes, but that's because they got something for free.

Carl: Exactly. Just like Rebecca. Rebecca is going to start feeling like she is getting something for free. She's getting answers to questions when she knows you are expecting her to make an effort before coming to her. After a few times, my guess is that Rebecca is going to figure this out on her own, and do something before coming to you for the answer.

It may take asking The Golden Question two or three times, maybe even five or six times, but at some point, it's going to change her behavior WITHOUT your telling her to change her behavior. That is the difference between her following your orders and taking the initiative to get the answer on her own.

So, let's say it works. Let's say she comes to you with a question, and after you ask, "What steps did you take to get the answer before coming to me?" Rebecca says, "I checked with two senior adjusters in the office."

Now you give Rebecca the answer and forget it.

6th Student: Then what?

Carl: Well, let's say the next three or four times she comes to you, and each time when you ask The Golden Question, she says she checked *with two senior adjusters in the office. Now you get to say, "Well Rebecca, you always do that. What EXTRA steps have you taken?" Of course she'll tell you none, and you can answer her question and let her go. The next few times she comes to you with only having checked with the senior adjusters and your response is "Well Rebecca, you always do that. What EXTRA steps have you taken?" It will not take Rebecca long to figure out she needs to do something in addition to checking with the two senior adjusters.*

So, after a few times of that, she finally says, "Well, first I checked with the two senior adjusters. Then I checked the FC&S books. I kind of got an answer, but not one I feel confident about."

Right now, believe it or not, without telling Rebecca to take initiative, she has gone and done a few steps on her own. Sure, you made her feel obligated, but nevertheless it was her own decision to do it.

Now, after a few more times of telling you she checked with the senior adjusters and the FC&S books, guess what you are going to start asking?

6th Student: *"Rebecca, you always check with them and the FC&S books. What EXTRA steps have you taken?"*

Carl: *Exactly. This process never stops. It just keeps building on the same question. But that's not even the best part. Once you have Rebecca checking five or six different resources and analyzing the situation on her own before she even comes to you, what will happen to the number of times she will even need to come to you?*

6th Student: *The number of times will drop because she will be finding the answers.*

Carl: *That's right. Not only will it drop, but Rebecca will gain knowledge and experience many times faster than the person who just comes to you asking questions, because she will have developed a process that she will use to figure out the answers.*

6th Student: *Will this really work?*

Carl: *Well, I have found it to work. It will take a good effort on your part. It couldn't hurt to try, because whatever you are doing now to create initiative isn't working. So it's worth a shot.*

7th Student: *What if Rebecca never feels obligated and just keeps taking the answers you give her.*

Carl: *Well, that's not possible because I know Rebecca and she is more dedicated to doing outstanding work than anyone I know. But let's go back to that lunch with your friend. After a few times of your buying lunch, your friend still doesn't feel obligated to buy it next time. What does that tell you?*

7th Student: *He's cheap.*

Carl: *Exactly. He's cheap. He's not going to change. He'll always be cheap. You can't change him. You can get him to buy lunch by saying, "you should buy this time, you cheapskate." That will work, but does it change him?*

7th Student: *No, you're just making him do it.*

Carl: *Right. So, if after three . . . maybe six . . . heck, maybe even ten times or so, your adjuster keeps taking the answers and going away, that tells you something. He has no desire to be outstanding. You'll never change him. He'll never learn to take the initiative, and he will always be looking for the easy way out.*

7th Student: *What would be your advice?*

Carl: *To forget it. Stop trying. He's not going to change. Just go back to telling him what to do and be happy if he does it. He's mediocre and will always be that way. Spend time teaching him to write a Reservation of Rights letter, or what to do when he receives a lawsuit. He'll never be an Awesome Adjuster, but you can at least make him a good technical adjuster. It doesn't mean he's useless, it means taking the initiative on matters is just not his thing. Find something else to work on. See if you can get him to stop hitting people with his claims hammer or something.*

(Long pause)

8th Student: *When's lunch?*

For you my reader, I hope the advice I gave my group of Claims Supervisors and Managers made sense. But I did promise a while ago that I would give a little piece of advice on how you could develop initiative in yourself, so here it goes.

First, you must ask yourself, do you want to be like Stann and Tom, or Dopey? If your answer is you would rather be more like Stann and Tom, then I have only a slight variation for you. The question is the same; the direction is just slightly different.

From this point forward, any time you find the need to ask your manager for the answer to something, ask yourself:

What steps did I take to get the answer before coming to my boss?

If you answer "nothing" and feel okay about it, go ask your boss your question and forget about it. The next time you have a question, again ask yourself, "What steps did I take to get the answer before coming to my boss?" and believe it or not, pretty soon you're going to feel obligated to yourself to take some initiative. And guess what . . . you WILL start changing your behavior. If you don't, then go work on your letter writing skills or something, because you'll never be like Stann or Tom.

That's it. That's just one small example of how easy it can be to create initiative in yourself, once you decide how you want people to see you.

SUMMARY

Awesome Adjusters are special people. They have the characteristics that separate them from the crowd.

Awesome Adjusters have positive attitudes that allow them to see the opportunities among all of the hard work. They look for ways to make something work, rather than looking at why it won't. They recognize that being a claims adjuster is a difficult job that not just anyone can do, but also appreciate the challenge that comes with that. They have the ability to recognize opportunity when they see it, because they know what it looks like.

Awesome Adjusters have time management skills that allow them to eliminate unnecessary work. They use communication skills such as nail down questions to help improve how much the customer understands and remembers. They avoid creating more work for themselves by answering calls instead of letting them roll into voice mail.

Awesome Adjusters have great interpersonal skills that allow them to gain cooperation from customers by focusing on how to help the customer instead of hitting them with the claims hammer. They know how to avoid arguments by listening to what the customer has to say and responding to the issue. They know their credibility comes from understanding the customer's point of view, not from the facts. They spend a little time letting the customer know that they are knowledgeable, experienced, want to do a good job, and are willing to do what it takes to make things go smoothly.

Awesome Adjusters are actively involved in raising their level of knowledge by seeking out information and helping others gain knowledge as well. They understand that learning is part of their job, and they participate in educating others in what they have learned.

Awesome Adjusters understand they are in the customer service business, and never lose sight of that. They look at each claim as an opportunity to help. They know their customers have been though something difficult and

require a high level of patience. They know very clearly that delivering customer service means meeting or exceeding expectations and taking the time
to set those expectations. They display empathy when appropriate and gain
credibility along the way.

Awesome Adjusters have the deep-rooted desire to do an excellent job, no
matter what that job is. They know that they will be judged not on what
they are capable of, but on what they do. They understand that the work
they produce is a reflection of them as people, and they want to be seen as
dependable and trustworthy. They know very well that they must earn the
right to be given more responsibility by doing an excellent job at all times.

Awesome Adjusters understand that they can never really be successful
while others around them struggle. Teamwork to them is more than just
pulling their own weight. It is helping others so that the whole team benefits. They know by helping others they will receive more in return than they
have given up. They are not in the "get rid of this guy if he's not my problem" business; they are in the "customer service" business.

Awesome Adjusters take initiative. Whether it is to find the answer to a
question before going to their supervisor, or whether it is to develop solutions
to problems that they see in the office, they take initiative. They feel obligated to do whatever they can to find answers and solutions before asking.
Because of this, they develop at an extraordinarily fast pace and enhance
their judgment ability. They know that being right is not nearly as important
as the efforts that they made to find the right answer.

Awesome Adjusters are here to stay. Technology has replaced many of the
claims functions that those of us who started in the business 25 years ago could
ever have imagined. From writing estimates to setting reserves, technology
continues to replace the daily functions of the claims adjuster. In the years
ahead, who knows, maybe investigations and negotiations will be done by
some clever computer program! But long after technology runs most of the
industry off, the Awesome Adjusters will still be around. They will be the ones
dealing with the difficult customers, when no one else could or wanted to.

171

OTHER PROGRAMS WRITTEN BY CARL VAN

Adjuster Soft-Skill

- Real-Life Time Management for the Claims Adjuster
- The 8 Characteristics of the Awesome Adjuster
- Negotiation Training for the Claims Adjuster
- Conflict Resolution for the Claims Adjuster
- Awesome Claims Customer Service
- Managing the Telephone
- Attitude & Initiative Training for the Claims Adjuster
- Empathy & Listening Skills
- Adjuster Organization – Managing the Desk
- Prepare for Promotion – Adjuster Leadership Training
- Teamwork Basics – No Adjuster is an Island
- Interpersonal Skills – Improving Team Member Relations
- Effective Recorded Statements
- Business Writing Skills for Claims Adjusters
- Beating Anxiety and Dealing With Anger – Help for the New Adjuster

Adjuster Technical

- Reservation of Rights Letters
- Coverage Denial Letters
- Excess Letters
- Essential Letters: Reservation of Rights; Denial; and Excess
- Policy Coverage Interpretation
- Advanced Policy Coverage Interpretation
- Adjusting Property Losses – Basic Overview
- CGL Policy – Basics

Manager Soft-Skill

- Time Management for Claims Supervisors and Managers
- Coaching and Teaching for Claims Supervisors and Managers
- Keys to Effective Presentations
- Teaching Your Adjusters the 8 Characteristics of Awesome Adjusters
- Motivating Your Claims Team
- Handling Difficult Employees
- The New Claims Supervisor
- Delegation Training for Supervisors and Managers
- Managing Change
- Team Training
- Leadership Skills for Claims Supervisors and Managers
- Preparing Effective Performance Appraisals
- Managing the Highly Technical Adjuster

9432591R0010

Made in the USA
Charleston, SC
14 September 2011